Joan's 90th Birthday, Álamos. Left to right: Ann Symons, Joan Gould Winderman, Jean Glattke, and Teri Arnold. Photo by Raül Rangel.

A Year of COVID in Álamos, Sonora, Mexico

Joan Gould Winderman

Handmade Paper Maker • Artist • Journalist • Photographer

Edited by Megan Gould Peterson

Alamos Press

Joan Gould Winderman
Handmade Paper Maker • Artist • Journalist • Photographer

Edited by Megan Gould Peterson

ISBN 978-1-953120-39-7

Front cover painting of Álamos Cathedral by Jim Wilson.
Back cover photo by Denise De La Peña.

For information, address joan.winderman@gmail.com

BLOG: grafinis.blog/Álamos-diary-2020-joan/

First Edition June 2022
Printed in the United States of America

Published by Álamos Press

An imprint of parkplacepublications.com

To my daughter, Megan.
Thank you for all your help.

Introduction

My 90th Birthday Party was in Álamos, Sonora, Mexico on March 8, 2020 at Teri's Bistro. It turned out to be an amazing day in so many ways. I saw more friends than I knew I had, ended up with gifts of more beautiful scarves then I had ever imagined having, was presented with a beautifully decorated cake, and was surprised with the gift of a lovely oil portrait of myself by Robyn Tinus. Life was perfect, until it suddenly was not. COVID 19 had arrived worldwide.

Americans who could, scattered, and I was alone (with Patricia for a short time) in the middle of a paradise with more than enough scarves for anyone and not nearly enough underpants, let alone masks. I wasn't complaining; I knew I was lucky. I found myself comparing my situation to Anne Frank, besieged by war, fearing death or even being seen. No, I didn't really have a problem. I lived in an Eden. I would write about it and take lots of pictures. I even for a time hoped it would last a year; it would make a better story.

I wanted people to know what the seasons are like in Àlamos. What the trees and tropical flowering vines are like. What fruit grows and when it becomes ripe. There was an abundance of all that within my walls. I worked hard researching the proper names for all the flowers I made into bouquets, knowing there would be women and men more knowledgeable than I reading my words. The bouquets, though, were for me to see what I could create with flowers every day.

Bird of Paradise, Plumeria, June.

This book is the result of almost one year of chronicling what I saw and did and thought about. My cats helped me keep the ball rolling along with whoever I could safely entice within earshot. I sent Rafaela and Carlitos home with pay so I could feel safe. After 6 months, though, I begged them to come back. I think they liked not working.

My daughter Megan came along with her graphic arts experience and volunteered just in time. Yes, we could do it all virtually from her perch in Solebury, Pennsylvania, near Philadelphia. Patricia Hamilton, from her perch in Pacific Grove, California, agreed to publish another book about her favorite Mexican town. So, I impulsively jumped into deep water again.

Profits for the sale of this book will go to Amigos de Educacion in Àlamos.

grafinis.blog/Álamos-diary-2020-joan/

Blog administrator Megan Gould Peterson.

Joan Gould Winderman
Álamos 2020-2021 Blog

Cupola on the roof of the casita where I reside half the time.

31 March 2020 Álamos

Podranea, Mexican Creeper, Thunbergia. Pot by Ellen Brown.

The temp is in the 90s today. I start pretending I am living in the garden of Eden.

Patricia leaves tomorrow on Volaris out of Obregon for CA. They canceled her a week ago but are announcing new flights which they keep delaying so we will see if she really goes. She tried to keep up her business here but with both my poor computer service and having to borrow my computer and then the offer of another flight she is now more determined to do it.

She can't really just take off work unless it is critical and I can't put pressure on her. She has informed me a lot about how to handle not getting infected and I am forever grateful to her for that.

Anyway, people here are aware that I am alone and are nearby. Another neighbor half a block away called to offer help. I had forgotten about them because I never see them. They have a nice place, a big truck and were firemen in CA but retired. She was the chief. And she seems very up on medical talk. I think they have to be EMT's.

I am paying Beto his full pay to come and work briefly and repair things for a few hours a week. So, I have help on call. I want to keep him alive. I will pay Fala her salary to stay home, got to keep all of us alive.

So, I have help on call. I want to have Fala come with a mask and gloves just to mop all the floors, for a short time once a week. She loves to wear a mask, wore one to get her pay. But not to cook, eat or even dust. I hear dusting just stirs things up. I will leave the big house closed and just live in the kitchen and casita. She can bring me things and pay bills.

I am bolting both doors and opening only the garage where I have set up a table to store things for 3 days before putting them in the garage refrigerator.

We still have plans for our girl get together once a week in the morning, each bringing our own sandwich. Too hot later. We are my birthday party girls and live within walking distance. I plan to walk shower wet like I do in Tucson on hot days.

I April 2020

Patricia just left in a cab for the Ciudad Obregon airport with her what she hopes is a final certified reservation out of Mexico. She is the most intrepid, smart, upbeat, prepared (traveling with a certified CA forest fire mask which she may be in danger of being attacked for) woman I know. We agreed she should camp in the airport UNTIL a plane leaves with her on it. She has peanut butter sandwiches, power bars, gloves. And in an emergency she will plead for a wheelchair (maybe my recommendation).

I was told by a Mexican friend that older people are so cherished that they are kept waiting for the last seat on the plane so they will be safe and incidentally all seated passengers will notice the special care given to them. Reports on her progress will be forthcoming.

It is a cloudless beautiful day and I am up ready to do battle with the Orange marauder. My cats huddle at the casita door predawn screeching away to let me know he is back. Why the three of them cannot take him out I do not know so I have to march out heavy footed screeching "get out you miserable ___________! You can fill in a different word every day. Sometimes I go back to bed but today I trudge up to the big house carefully grabbing all the rusty iron railings I cemented in place trying not to kick the cat kids who get under my feet. I cannot hurt myself as the three of them would make a soft landing. Providing they stay together. And they are of a mind.

So I fill their bowl and place it just outside the screen door where I sit with my coffee next to a basket of pebbles ready to fire at the first sign of the marauder. You can see by the pic that they are usually never far from their food. It is relaxing to sit and drink my coffee while on guard duty. Something important to do.

Yesterday, Chuy came by with a package of 90 dark roast coffee pods. He ordered it on line from Mercado Libre. It didn't arrive the next day but within a few weeks. I suggested he try a few more things to see what happens. Can't catch fish without a hook in the water.

No word from Patricia yet. That could mean she got on a plane. Ann said that Lorna, where she had been renting, said she could come back for free and stay there alone to keep from infecting others.

So today the girls below came for our weekly Coffee Klatch. Each week we improve it as we learn how to and discuss the latest. We all seem to be listening to the same Doctor in New York telling us how to keep safe. Very soothing.

Teri.

Jean.

Ann.

Melanie drove in two days ago from Sonoita, AZ to get her dogs and let her house sitters go. She said the roads were empty but they were stopped 40 miles outside of town on the only road in) and were told they could not drive into Àlamos. That was good news for us but not for them. She pleaded with them in her best Spanish and after calling ahead to check that she really had a house they relented but told her she could not leave her house. Now that they have their dogs they are talking about driving back out.

We talked about groups forming like ours that can safely meet while obeying all the best practices. I seem to be the only one who is barring her maid. I will see how long I can keep that up.

3 April 2020

Bulletin from Patricia. She made it to San Diego and is now holed up in a hotel waiting for a flight to Monterey, California.

From Patricia, April 2: *Believe it or not! Volaris flight without incident. Five immigration booths open — I was the only immigrant passing through. The Uber driver said my fare was the only one he had from the CBX crossing today. I'm in the Marriot Residence downtown — a few people walking their dogs on otherwise deserted streets. Hotel is quiet — no one. I'm glad to be home in this strange ghost town.*

Haven't had time to freshen up so no photo today. I have been fighting my aparata all morning. Trying for structure, my weakness.

That roasted onion, garlic and tomato sauce smells so good it doesn't need to be eaten. Got lots in the freezer in case this situation gets worse. If I survive, I will have a tomato sauce party.

Cats have calmed down this morning but are ever vigilant. I doubt we have intimidated the Orange devil. I found him after all food was put away under the yellow car waiting last night.

Millions of baby mangoes on the giant tree, but thousands are blown to the ground daily and yet I expect I will have hundreds of ripe ones to fillet and freeze in June. I have never filleted a mango. Hope Fala is alive and back here doing what she has always done so well. And me too, even though I have only ever eaten them.

Below: *Robyn Tinus painting of Álamos from her balcony looking down in better days. Although it looks the same today from a distance. A bit emptied out of people though.*

Chuy scored again yesterday. He arranged to have coffee arrive from Amazon or Mercado Libre not sure. He seemed to think he could rest on his laurels but I quickly ordered 6 reading glasses no. 3.00. Mine are crippled, broken, scratched, etc. All 8 of them. The box is sitting there for three days now to decontaminate.

Zucchini plants.

So glad to see I still have zucchini and eggplant coming on. Maybe it will last thru the duration.

Melanie and Richard arrived here from Sonoita a week ago after being stopped at the police station in Navojoa. No cars allowed on the only road in to Álamos. She had to fight her way in with her best Spanish. Now she has announced that after resting up by being quarantined she will leave her maid in the house and drive back out with her dogs on Sat. She lives on 30 acres in Sonoita, Arizona, there so no problem being isolated.

Ahhh, plans that will have to wait. I have no interest in starting up something new.

4 April 2020

Marc called today from San Miguel to say that his live-in girlfriend Luz Marie from Mexico is hearing talk around town that the Americans are sending the virus down to Mexico and the campesinos are enraged. There may be trouble. They are outside the city and plan to hunker down for the long haul. It is good to live with someone who hears the gossip.

Beto came by yesterday to get his pay for staying home, which he isn't, I am sure. He has a lively social life with a second wife, four kids in his father's house with extended family. He doesn't think ahead. I told him he needs to stay home, wash his hands and wear a mask. He said he can't stay home, too much to do like paying his monthly cell phone bill. Besides he said he has no masks. It may be a typical response of the working class. I want to take him in, lock the door and keep him because he is so smart, strong and can fix everything. Chuy and I are paying him his weekly salary regardless, not much but he has been living on it.

Just got a Patricia email, she got into San Francisco yesterday and drove herself south to Pacific Grove. Safe at home. She emailed that she mailed our letters. Now she will be hiding out for two weeks. Phew!

These gorgeous bulbs! Why have they never bloomed again? Every year I have been bringing them down for Christmas then planting them in the yard. Patricia said the reason is that they need the time to store up energy, that is a long time. Well, now that I know what it takes for me or someone better keep it up. She and her husband published a book about growing houseplants. It is amazing what you can learn down here. Think what else I might learn if I could speak more Spanish.

Ann stopped me in the street to get this photo. I was walking to the ATM in my new dangled birthday scarf disguise. I read that just covering the face with a veil stops you from touching the face. Hard to see though, you need an armed Guard and guide.

5 April 2020 – COVID 19 Domingo Abril

Woke up with everything hurting, despaired for a while. Then made and sipped hot coffee, now nothing hurts and my head is clear for a change. Must thank ____ for small blessings. Good to have my cat company eager and oblivious to everything but their world. This morning there are only two and one is dragging a dead mouse to their breakfast bricks. Stories are more interesting when they include surprise elements.

There, I said it, and the orange marauder appeared brazenly on the portal staring straight at me. I yelled something and he/she backed away to little whimpers from my scattering darlings. They have a protector and she is me. Not all-seeing somehow because the dead mouse disappeared while I was clearing the stage of the cat food.

Now and I am in place with a good view of the stage and ready to begin the second act now that things have settled down.

One by one they are creeping back, looking for their lines.

Intermission, I guess.

Where was I? Yesterday I crawled on the floor to vacuum the kitchen/window sitting room/office area and placed sheets over the rug. Now my two snowy white sheet-covered couches are draped cozily like in an Arabian movie. Why am I doing this? I can clean by shaking a sheet out.

It is exciting to sit in my Apache Lake cabin 50-year old swivel chair surveying 180 degrees of my kingdom. Periodically a few cats surmount the two-foot parapets staring into the distance ever mindful of my presence in case their food source should reappear or disappear.

A Studio with a View, that could be the name of my next story. Always buy intense colored sheets in case you are ever trapped in a lockdown to dramatize your situation.

I have been seeing many versions of homemade masks on the Internet. This intrigued me because I have itchy eyes, and nose and facial allergies. Maybe spring will be over before the pandemic hits Àlamos, in the meantime I am trying out

designs. God knows I have enough scarves, old turtle necks, and tiny dish towels.

This apparition has come full circle after being gifted with him/her one day by Ron Slaughter when he left town. I have kept her/him around because I felt she/he had much to offer that was not readily apparent.

First, I had to smash one of the last of my first marriage gifts, a china teacup. Arzberg to be exact. Choosing that design for my wedding pattern was I believe the first indication that I might have what is called taste.

WHAT YOU CHOOSE IS WHAT YOU ARE

I did that because this figure needed eyes, it had none. Picking through the shards I chose the ones you see, not creating an expression of maleness or femaleness particularly, not humbleness nor hopefulness. I have left them in place for 25 years thinking one day I would discover what I was looking for.

She/he came close to being tossed into the fireplace one night but we went to bed as a chill set in. Several times I tried draping junk rosaries and cheap necklaces on him/her. They are still there waiting for just the right one to get the look. What look? Well, that's the thing, I really don't know.

My friend Jean gifted me with this fine hemmed linen square. It had to be displayed, but where? It was probably made to cover a silver candy dish? The jeweled butterflies are awesome. It has covered the gamut, overinflated ceramic Cammy-made angels, topping a pitcher of lemonade, etc. I recently dropped it over this creature's head, and Voilá! a penitent with precious jeweled earrings.

The reason it is now beside the cat dish in front of the screen door is … I don't really know.

6 April 2020

I was attacked at 5:00 a.m. by one of the cats staring at me and scratching at my door this morning.

I watched the Brooklyn hospital CNN news video this morning. Horrendous. The last place I would want to be is in a hospital, especially because I wouldn't be in the running to be saved.

On a good day (last year in the Emergency Room at TMC in Tucson twice), it was scary having blood taken twice, being given a drip of something, wheeled away for tests, shivering, waiting and being poked and prodded. I thought then it was crowded.

I remember Grampa saying he didn't want a pacemaker because he would just have to die of something else. I remember all of his pithy sayings; well everything he said was pithy.

I had a shock yesterday while roaming around in the yard. I came upon The Marauder asleep high up on top of the Amazon delivery boxes on the laundry table where The Cats take turns napping. He didn't budge, had missed lunch and breakfast, but seemed to be moving in regardless. I guess I haven't scared him off yet. Time to rethink this war effort.

This morning I walked to Chuy's house, unlike Little Red Riding Hood with a basket of tomatoes and a giant zucchini, more healthy fare. While waiting for the gate to open I pushed my vegetables thru a hole at the bottom of the gate. By the time Chuy got there the large zucchini was gone. His guard dog was starting to eat it.

Undeterred, we took off up a slight hill uncharacteristically recently cement paved. Great place to walk 6 ft. apart. Chuy tried to soothe me by saying not to worry, he would scrub it carefully before he ate it so it wouldn't be wasted.

It seemed like a promising morning, cool, sporadic gently dropping tiny drops of rain freshening the air, when I spied his missing other guard dog. He had gotten out last week and was brought back and had recently gotten out again.

He was followed by what looked like a pack of dogs or a cult.... they wanted him back and followed us. Why?? He is a he. Why would a pack of he's need another one? Well, we were close to my house so Chuy started teasing him to follow us, it was difficult with the pack coming at us and barking.

We arrived at my house. I opened the garage and shooed both of them inside. We had talked before of my needing a watchdog who barks. Chuy's need to keep his best dog from getting away at will fits in with what I need.

He (got to find out the dog's name) is still here. I hear him banging on the screen doors periodically which I have blocked with chairs. Actually, I have blocked all my doors with things, no inside locks.

He is very smart, trained to guard, but has let me into Chuy's compound now for over a year. I think he will give up, too smart for futility.

Phew. I just managed to go down to the casita to pee with him following me. He stayed with me till I got back, checking to see that I shut the door properly and trotted off. He IS smart. Covering all activity looking for advantage but not wasting time or effort. Sitting here by the window I can see and watch his comings and goings.

I have satisfied his hunger drive, now the sex drive will be harder. He is used to living with cats. WAIT .... maybe the Maurader will think twice about returning!!!

How do old ladies, used to living with dogs, manage to live with a houseful of cats? Well, they don't. The cats just move in while the old ladies do nothing.

Now there is another big problem...

7 April 2020

I guess the sound effects are in place now, I hear howling and crying, the drama continues. They are in the background and only intermittent by the way. Today there is no interloper, I am not surprised though, as there has been a cast change.

Yesterday the new dog got out when I was purchasing my first delivery of homemade "tortillas integral" in the garage. He would not come back. I called but had forgotten to ask his name.

Later with a description of where I thought he was headed—to the bitch in heat—Chuy managed to coax the now named Prieto back.

Then I heard Prieto started howling like a wolf a few times. He really has nothing to howl about. I am glad I read *The Life of Pi*. I remember thinking if I am ever in a lifeboat with a tiger I will know exactly how to survive. Carefully.

This morning I had to strategize how I was going to feed the factions while trying to keep the peace. The good news is that it will take up most on the day which would otherwise be spent wondering when the Pandemic will hit Álamos.

Prieto slept all night guarding the entrance to the casita. The cats used to do that sometimes. They have disappeared. So, I went up to the kitchen with him and searched for disposable food he might like. Chuy said don't worry he is a Mexican dog and will eat anything, "Feed him cat food!"

Oh, no, I painstakingly have their food set. So, I dug out old frozen tortillas, and the Chinese Egg-flavored wheat noodles of which I don't want to ever have to eat all of. And a fresh egg and some BLT bacon grease which I was saving for the end of the world. After cooling and presenting the mess it was gone in a second.

He was inside and they minus Mia were outside eating.

Get this, I had to entice him into the kitchen to eat as I figured he was easier to remove than three cats, then I gave the cats their food while he was inside. They had appeared as if by magic while he was in the kitchen. Only two of them came to their bowl. Dan was obviously alarmed and caught my eye every time I appeared at a window to check the goings on.

10 April 2020

As I roam with my coffee looking over the rainwashed garden, in my garage sale 3 Donna Karan black wool over-sized now bathrobe, I am so at peace. It feels like we just survived a heavy storm. We, the cats and I. All night the howling, banging crashing and racing was Prieto tearing around responding to the call of a female in heat. I was terrorized in the dark. He had aroused other dogs and it sounded like an invading army.

I decided to do what Chuy had suggested, "if it gets to be too much, just open the garage door." Prieto led me there as if getting out that door was HIS plan. I opened it and crept back to bed. In the morning the cats were at the casita again, reunited after scattering to the winds for three days. They were not to be seen but had been just waiting it out. They didn't seem to be judging me. They know nothing of my involvement. We are back to what I hope will be an uneventful isolation period.

Dan looks up at me after finishing what he wants for breakfast as if to say, "Good to be back."

Now the only marauder is the original Marauder who took advantage of yesterday's chaos to get a quick snack. I guess he is used to fighting to be fed.

Mexican Creeper, Cosmos, Thunbergia, Rose, Nasturtium, Duranta, Petunia.

It was such a relief to wake up with my cat kids scratching at the door this morning. They are back and bumping into each other with the anticipation of a morning meal as usual. The past few days are gone and they have weathered it. No recriminations or no regrets, just content to continue on.

Actually, I feel the same way. That was just a storm and now a new day is here. I watch them wiggle pleasantly at their bowl for position, occasionally let out a tiny ssssss at whoever is irritating them and subside patiently to eat with renewed effort.

They are so alert. I watch Dan perk up to inaudible sounds of what I guess are birds moving and lizards flicking. I read that a cat's hearing is off our charts. It is like being able to hear the concert while only reading the notes.

Thank god for cats. In a pandemic they have special attributes which I might not otherwise have taken the time to notice. Lots of time now. They are self-possessed, focused on self-preservation, and fortunately unable to penetrate or unlock man-erected barriers—yet are able to leap over them.

They come to visit with me briefly the same way they come to visit their food bowl periodically to make sure it is still there.

This is forcing me to focus on Hope. There is more of that than all the things that are hopeless. That is the good news. It looks to me that carrying on as safely as I can and choosing only what seems most important is good anyway. I am forced to make hard choices. And again, the act of choosing allows me to see who I am.

14 April 2020

This has been ano ther interesting morning and now into the cat lunchtime. I get to sit on guard duty again. For some reason I am not tired so I will push on. First, I woke up energized, pulled on my disguise, and whipped off for a walk going past Chuy's house to give Rosy my new batch of Sarah's tomato rice soup. She gave me the recipe once when I pulled experience on her and suggested that she might want to make Ratatouille with her garden vegetables. I had to take it to be polite but it turned out to be the equal to, if not better than, my recipe. Her recipe requires a pressure cooker but I managed to dumb it down to putting water in a big pan, lots of rice, tomatoes, green peppers, garlic, onions, herbs available, parsley and chicken broth. Then cooking it without a lid till it looks and tastes the way I wanted it. Soup, stew, casserole, additions or not, etc. Lovely but you need a garden ready to harvest. I also took her my pretty good tiny batch of ricotta.

What I found was another Dr. Doolittle sitting in a chair near his front door surveying his garden of Eden. He was covered in clamoring dogs all wanting attention, spitting, growling, fighting, snapping, and all whining to get it. All showing off. No Prieto, gone but not missed apparently.

The other female guard dog, a black puppy wild to be part of the group, heedless of the danger. And the tiny aggressive chihuahua who thinks he is the king of the roost.

I took off and stopped at a tiny well-run tienda on my way home and found lots of what I need. A report on CNN this morning suggested that people get at least 4,000 steps a day exercise to keep strong. This walk uses 2,000 of that number. Hope I can keep it up as it is safe, smooth, and no dog packs so far.

As is my way, I started to do many things at once. Cleaned out the refrigerator while looking for the recipe again for Mark Bittman's no-knead bread which I had put together yesterday and set in the cold oven to rise for 18 hours with the lid on. Not looking too risen, I decided to leave it...

Then I heated a new batch of olding milk to try out making lime ricotta. Lemon ricotta is lovely, why not lime? No lemons now, but lots of limes. Alas, the flavor is too limy. It didn't clot like it should either, so I added some vinegar and left it. I am trying to get a feel for when the temperature is just right. Not there yet but even when it isn't perfect it still can be eaten and isn't wasted.

In Mexico the milk often doesn't last till the expiration date and I need alternatives. Free materials to play with.

This reminds me of how I started making paper. Try everything to see what works. The results can be startling, that in my case has determined my style.

Well, the bread is done but is only half an inch high. Crust is good, too much crust though, and the color is strange. I carefully picked lots of thyme leaves growing bountifully and tossed them in with the dough and extra walnuts. I see now thyme turns dough a soft lilac color. Didn't know that. Maybe it was caused by the proximity to Easter??

Anyway, it is crusty, with not much bread and mildly aromatic. Crusty is more important than bready. I will keep on trying as it is easy and I am tired of tortillas.

16 April 2020

Have you ever heard of Tiny Dead Ant Coffee? I invented it. My precious honey is kept in a tightly closed glass container. Lately I have taken to storing it on a window ledge outside because fewer tiny ants seem to discover it there. They are so tiny you can barely see them, I guess because they don't move, which has led me to conclude they are probably dead. I now add them and it to my breakfast coffee after noticing their dead presence hasn't affected the flavor. Nutrition comes in many shapes and sizes. I intend that this will become part of my regular diet as a reminder after this Pandemic is over.

18 April 2020

I cannot believe how beautiful it is here now, Spring, eighties and nineties, AC and fans working and sitting on the portal one would think there was no chaos in the world.

Celebrating Easter in my Easter outfit — a nightgown with 90th Birthday Scarf by Ann Gallagher.

In the past when I read about disasters: pandemics, floods, hurricanes, tornadoes, and shocking gun violence it was always somewhere else. Now it is nearing everywhere I am or want to be. I guess it is my turn.

The news around the world does drown out the stupidity in American politics. It might even force Americans to look at what are really the most critical dangers facing mankind today. Those dangers are going to overwhelm us while we fritter away the little time we have left to do what we can do to reverse what looks like the inevitable.

In a way I can accept our pandemic if it changes the conversation. I don't really need to live to see what wins out. How life, if there will be any left on earth, will become changed from organic based to algorithms to a new species. I wouldn't be able to cope.

There won't be a place for grandmothers in rocking chairs. Speed and data will be where it is at. You will have to grow up with it to understand it. Harari says that the coming change (if it isn't the apocalypse) will be more radical than the changes we live with now would be to early cave men.

Day lily, Larkspur, Jasmine.

Prieto was back. He was with two buddies who waited for him down the street. Would you have pushed food through the bars—or let him back in??

Report from Patricia Hamilton, April 20, 2020, email to Jean Glattke

Patricia trying the new outdoor shower.

Thought you would like to know that I have contracted the Coronavirus — fortunately, it's a very mild case.

About 6 days after I left Álamos, I began having symptoms that I initially attributed to allergies (slight sore throat), change of climates (chills), and a common cold (stuffy nose and congested chest). Then I experienced sudden symptoms I couldn't explain, such as only one day of diarrhea, intermittent fevers, and acute aches I'd never before had.

I searched online for personal experiences with the virus and ran across a doctor who said that the majority of people who get it will experience only mild symptoms. Today, I read an article that said some people with it actually have no symptoms.

Just FYI, in case any of you might be experiencing similar bodily aches. I didn't have any fever until the last few days, off and on again, about 3 times now. It's unknown if I'll be immune when this is over, so I intend to continue to follow the washing, social distancing, et al. I'm actually glad I got it — now I know I'm not going to die from it — well, not this go around anyway. First job I did when I got home was update the documents in my End of Life Binder, just in case!

In Monterey County we are instructed to first call our physician, describe our symptoms, and they make the decision. COVID tests are generally not available. I described my symptoms, over time, and was told, yes, and to stay at home, rest and hydrate — and to call 911 if I developed any trouble breathing.

That hasn't happened, and I'm feeling much better every day. Greatly relieved to have — so far — dodged that bullet. I understand relapses have occurred.

I'm happy to hear all are fine — yes, I do believe I may have picked it up at the Obregon airport — so many people crowded together in the waiting to board area, and again in the boarding line, no social distancing at all — I was about the only one with a mask and while I wiped down a lot with the disinfectant cloth I carried, there were still a lot of surfaces I didn't — plus the plane was fully booked. Also, the airport in Tijuana was very busy. Oh, well! Take care, Patricia

Monterey County Weekly has a story on their local Americans trying to get home from abroad. It begins with Patricia's tale.

21 April 2020

I started up Galeana this morning for my walk and came upon what looks like Cecy's new project. She has built a barbecue for rooftop parties. Will you ever return to making us all as beautiful? WE NEED HAIRCUTS.

Then on to Teri's kitchen window where I can always find her. She doesn't seem to mind that she has closed Teresita's Bistro and now has lots of time on her hands. Wonder why? We got into a contest about who was wearing the most interesting outfit we had slept in last night. Mine was the most interesting but hers cost the most.

Very early this morning, I got it together to make a new attempt to produce a better-looking Mark Bittman no-knead 24-hour loaf of bread. I work best using the trial and error method. This time, better instant yeast, dissolving the yeast in warm water first, starting early enough to set it in a sunny window to get it started rising, and avoiding the 1/4 cup of fresh thyme leaves now that I know they turn bread dough lavender. Can't get away with that now Easter is behind us.

I am crossing my fingers that it won't end up looking like something a camel would leave behind in the desert like my last effort.

The new wrinkle is a quarter cup of carefully cleaned, dried cilantro seeds (coriander), and oven-dried powdered parsley leaves. Lots of things out there to choose from.

More later when I take it out of the oven early tomorrow. I think there is a lot of leeway but we shall see. I like stretching leeway as I have a better chance of being surprised.

I've recently learned of a way out of here by car when things settle down a bit but timing will be so important. Out of the frying pan into the fire. So far, no credible reports of the virus here but no reports of testing either.

The military is supposedly stationed at all roads into Álamos and not allowing anyone in but .... how stringent they are, who knows. Lots of people with masks moving around on the streets. I wish we could jump a decade or two when supposedly we (the U.S.) will have in place virtual surveillance of everyone and have the ability to spot the first signs of danger both internally and among the population. Scary to think about but necessary for the survival of future generations.

We Americans living here should benefit by the past experience of early Spanish settlers who lived in large fortress like enclaves protected from attack by disease and the poor always a danger because of living conditions.

I am behind walls and windows barred with gardens still producing edible produce. And a well. So far, I am keeping it up, at least enough of it.

Gloria, Cosmos, Petunia, Duranta.

22 April 2020

Right now, I am sitting here with the lovely yeast smell wafting from the not yet burning bread wondering if all is well in other parts of the world, not just here, but poised to act just in case. Like this morning, when I swiped a precious wine glass to the floor as I passed by frantically looking for the batteries to goose my timer clock in case I have to make a judgment about timing whatever it is in the gauge-less oven. That smells so good.

I JUST TOOK THE BREAD OUT (coriander). Not purple! It looks like a one-inch high blond female hard piece of camel dung and tastes lovely with olive oil dribbled on top.

Well, my sail just went up, tomorrow will be our first 100-degree day of the year. That would not be so bad but it might continue on till September... when the humidity will match it. Normally I would have left Àlamos for Tucson but need to g et this room ready to live in.

28 April 2020

Just got freshened up to see if it will be worth surviving this. Today my eyes are not so itchy and red thank god.

I showered and washed my clothes in buckets of water out in the sun just like I used to do when we first came to Álamos. Can't wait till my pool rain water collection system can collect enough rain so I can waste it. Wasting things I have too much of is my favorite thing to do.

This afternoon I look forward to washing my portal, plants and scaring my cats with a shower. They like to lay around on damp shady bricks afterwards.

I think all I need besides good health to be happy now is plenty of water, soap, rubber gloves, AC, WiFi and freezers full of things that need to be eaten or else thrown away, Friends, Bittman homemade bread. That is a lot actually and I feel bad that so many people don't even have that.

Ann Symon, drive-by conversation.

I just read that the U.S. now has more than a million cases of the Coronavirus and Álamos appears to have none, or are there cases that go unreported? Am I in the right place or will we soon have our turn?

The good news is that the Pandemic could be what gooses the world, including the United States, to wake up to the reality that there is real change going on whether we choose to face it or not and we don't have time left. Those of us who survive will have to embrace even more drastic change and cooperate or we will be swept away.

I cannot imagine having to live through what is coming even if we beat this one Pandemic. Hope checking out is easier. My impression is that those who are stepping up and making change happen are not going to wait for everybody. That means that everybody is going to be left behind.

Marigold, Thunbergia, Nasturtium, Petunia, Trumpeta, Clerodendron.

We need to listen to the people who see what is coming and are preparing. Yuval Noah Harari, Gates, Obama, Greta, Nancy Pelosi, Fauci, German Chancellor Olaf Scholz, President Biden (he's trying), many Democrats, Jared Diamond, Jane Fonda, and no Republicans. These are all the people I can think of right now but I am going to start making a list and add to that from now on because there are thousands and I will need to Google people.

Focusing on who is stepping up is more important than making fun of who isn't.

30 April 2020

This may be my Year of Magical Thinking. It amuses me to think that if I take the scissors with me when I shower outside when it is 100 degrees then not only will I not leave a mess to clean up but by slowly clipping away at my dandelion seed head of hair it will stay perfectly even and stylishly short forever. The point is to never cut more than ¼ inch anywhere at a time. Of course, ¼ inch in the hot sun varies. One might not be always alert to what one is doing on any given day, in this hot sun. But one has to take that chance and maybe no one is paying attention anyway because we all have more important things on our minds.

My outdoor shower.

I will have to remember to take a selfie occasionally to see how I am doing. I wish I had an outside mirror set up. I am beginning to wish for a lot more things after listing what little I really need. I couldn't do without my Alexa, even though I only ask her to play the songs of José José when I exercise.

I would like to have an iPhone that allows me to make phone calls for free. I lost that privilege when it was stolen Jan. 4th. I got a new one with insurance but it cannot be activated to make calls till I visit in person a Verizon outlet in the states. Who knows when that will happen?

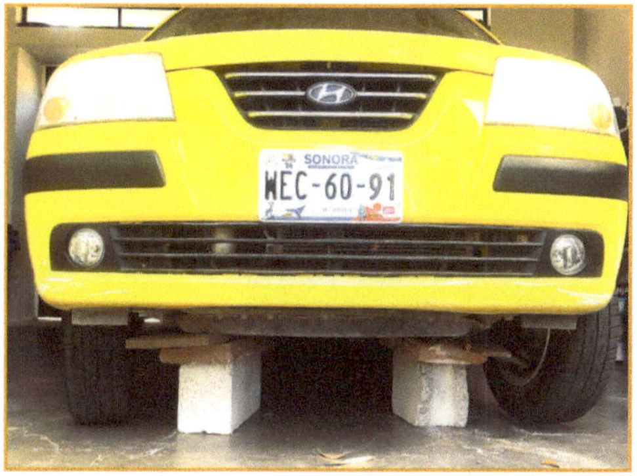

My car now "almost" up on blocks and things.

Beto self-distancing.

1 May 2020

I never looked better, guess why? I keep getting compliments about looking fabulous. Not my arms, legs, face, neck, back, skin looks fabulous. WHY? You never see those things!!! WHY?

Guess, you never see those things because they don't look fabulous!! Just hide them.

The next thing to go is my eyes. Do you think that is why Anna Wintour always wears sunglasses? She claims bad eyes...

How to look fabulous.

Hanging out in the shade on the steps of # 6 Toluca.

Friends Passing by ...

Friends visiting, socially distant, clockwise from top left: Ann, Rod, Nicole, and Jean. We all had a great visit, even got to see two other expats walking by. One we had to instruct in the new dress code.

2 May 2020

Manuel 93 years young, all dressed up at the door for his pay this morning. He walks maybe a mile to get here. No cane. He is looking really good. Earle would be proud of me for keeping him on all this time. If Earle decided to come back alive it might just be to see Manuel at 93 dressed in a new hat. In that way they were not alike. Earle liked to wear what looked like Manuel's old hats.

He asked me who sweeps away the leaves and I told him Beto uses the sopladora (not in dictionary but used locally for leaf blower) and just blows them all into the compustera (a word used in my house for compost). He laughed. Manuel likes to push them around with his ancient broom, collect them carefully and set them outside for the daily trash truck.

He asked about Fala, "Does she still clean?" When I told him that I did the cleaning he laughed. I guess he thought that was a joke.

Still no known cases of the virus here.

This is the first time I've seen a cat posing here. Has he any idea it is not a good fit? His image doesn't seem to be behind this action. Is he laying an egg? If this Pandemic lasts long enough, I may figure this out.

New Bandera arrangement, named after the colors of the Mexican flag.
Potter Paul Bernhardt, Wayne, PA.

5 May 2020

This is the still nameless slut who snuck food for months when I couldn't get rid of her. I had to capture her and get her fixed and take care of her and feed her till she was on her own. Then she hung around, hung on Dan's every word, snuggled and wiggled all over him, followed him — which he tolerates to this day — during the time his true love turned nasty, probably because she was also hanging out at night with a bad crowd.

I still have not named her, shun her, talk about her behind her back when I see her posing shamelessly in front of him. Mia spits at her when she gets too close and occasionally takes a swipe at her. Not that she appears to be jealous, but just because she enjoys torturing the obsequious little bitch.

I know how she feels, I get cranky once in a while, too. I never call her to come and eat.

No, I never call Mia either because she has taken her shittiness out on me also. I enjoy holding their food up and making a point of announcing dinner for Dan alone, then making them wait till he arrives. I notice that even when they are far away, when I call him over and over, they both come. Like they don't have names. Well, one doesn't.

13 May 2020

So, I walk in my garden now just looking at things much like my cats do. They are known to attack what they see though and devour it. Actually, I do too but there isn't much to eat at this time of year.

From top, clockwise: Baby grapefruit, baby lemon, baby mango, baby lime.

Lately I have noticed that many of my trees are full of green fruit already! The lime trees have tiny green balls, the Meyer lemon tree, bigger green balls, and the grapefruit even bigger ones. I had never noticed this as I am usually gone in April. It always pissed me off having to leave before the limes were ripe. But then, they do fruit twice during the year and some are ripe anytime. They aren't as scripted as are other trees, I think.

I will get to see when the mangoes ripen in June/July this year. In the past I have only seen the mounds of frozen filleted mangoes that greet me in October. There are no guavas showing now but they become ripe in Sept/Oct. And the bananas are still pumping them out, the fourth stem is producing right now and they will start all over next year.

Left: green mangoes; center: baby grapefruit; right: baby oranges.

22 May 2020

Ann Symons came by today to tell me about the news of Àlamos but first I had to tell her she looked like an exotic South American Parrot. Stunning. Don't you agree? She just bought a house and hasn't even painted it yet she knows what is going on all over town. Even making things happen herself.

She and Annette Hinman are helping to keep Àlamos going right now. How many single women and widows are living in Àlamos? The best estimate I can make is that it is around 45.

I was sitting by my rainwater pool garden in the early morning sun talking to Marc in San Miguel when Mia my crabby cat wandered over and leaned heavily against my back and wiggled. Caught off guard for a second, I responded with a sigh and thought briefly, "how nice she is letting me know it is time for breakfast," then she bit me.

Fala came to visit and when I told her that Mia bit me she got out her cat clippers and cut her nails. Hope that keeps Mia from biting me ever again.

Fala climbed up and cut some beautiful Plumeria branches.

I am getting pretty good at making very small leis. I wish I was on a beach in Hawaii tho doing this. I made a lei and sent a photo to the poor Hawaiians Lisa and Chuck sheltering in Pennsylvania.

1 June 2020

I sit here looking out at the yard and thinking I feel like I am on a train watching the scenery go by. Well, some doves, birds, leaves, cats, flies, clouds, butterflies, wind, flowers and palm fronds do go by.

My first salad from my indoor garden.

Now that I have 25 new underpants, my Tucson condo has been freshly cleaned, my indoor lettuce is 1.5 inches high, my haircut is a week old and my eyes are no longer red and itchy I have a new lease on life. At the very least I am ready to do battle. BUT my computer is still out of whack, and I am out of my best lipstick. If you feel like driving to Àlamos bring a tube of Clinique Kiss.

I was feeling the loss of the niceties I was beginning to enjoy since retiring and was starting to feel a little wimpy. But then I realized that I could control the story I tell myself, I could switch perspectives. This is a pretty easy one, one of the wimpy ones.

I am lucky to be old, in relatively good health, have a house (well two), enough money to take care of my needs, etc, etc. AND I have lots of time on my hands, lots.

I have been hearing girls talk about getting pedicures lately with some feeling of at least now after all this time I can enjoy that little pleasure. I was shocked as it has been only two and a half months and it is okay to enjoy that personal a service? Buying groceries is one thing but being touched?

I quit doing my own pedicures many years ago when I was working because I had to go to parties, travel, shop, join clubs, go to the library, go to the doctor and dentist, make beds, mop floors, invite people over for dinner, i.e., there was no time, especially in Álamos.

And I was finding I didn't bend too well anymore. It hurt to get down on the floor.

But now I have nothing but time and have to spend lots of time exercising just to keep moving and out of pain. So why not give myself a safe pedicure and devote enough time to it so it isn't a strain. Take hours, days. Try and see what I could make happen.

Ha! I did it. But I won't tell how long it took.

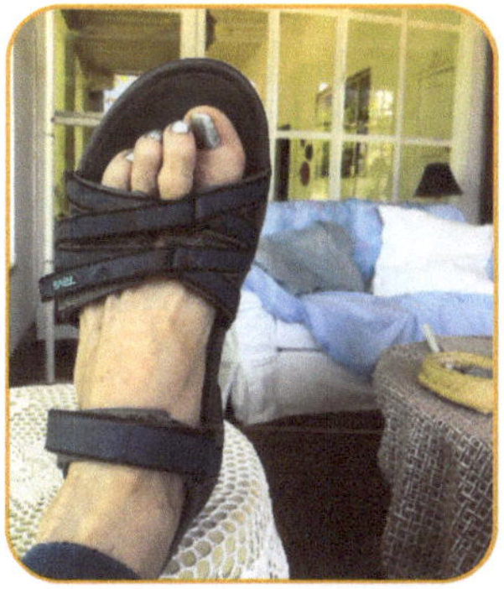

But I will tell you there are some tricks. Start training ahead of time just so you can get down on the floor, bend, grasp nail files, and not spill polish. Start slow and spend lots of time scrubbing, rinsing, drying, creaming, filing just like they do in Salons. That is half the battle. Anyone can do those things.

Trim nails short so there is not much to polish, choose any old non-bright color because people don't waste a lot of time looking at pedicures. Clean off dribbles. And it helps if you are missing a nail which can be covered with a bandaid. More than one though looks careless.

I only showed my left foot as the other does have toes that bend in the wrong direction which don't really look so good.

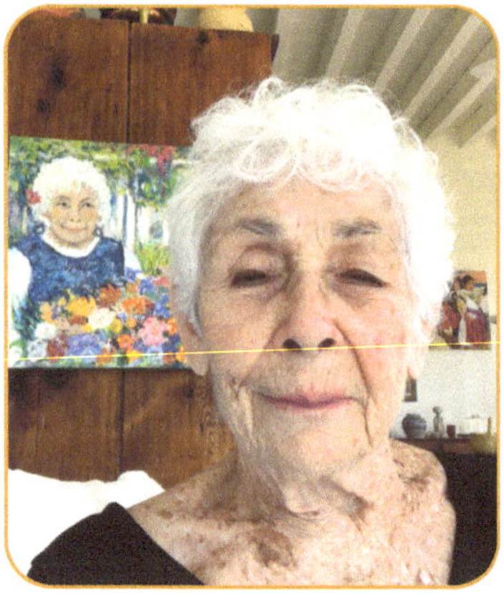

I am slipping back to feral which I can do so easily since toeing the line has always been hard on me. We got feral when we first came down here in the hot rainy season when we were camping out.

Mexican Creeper.

I am reduced to frying up whatever looks edible. My eggplants are all yellow and look like another species. I am frying them in cracker crumbs and pretending they are Grandpa's fried oysters. It works. Fried cardboard would be good too.

About 9 a.m., late and hot for me, I started out just to see how far I could get. First, I stopped at Chuy's gate and he came hobbling out with his bad foot (fascia or something) really frustrated by not being able to walk. Then I went on up his slightly inclined paved shady street to Linda's house to bug them from outside. If anyone survives it will be them. They built their entire house themselves with very little help. After that it was downhill, an outside shower, and Teri's Bistro supplies divine gazpacho and coconut flan.

This is where I put visitors to keep them safe at a distance in my kitchen air conditioning. Recognize Teri?

I had to make this sign because often I am unaware when I'm in the kitchen or casita of people at the front door.

I keep takeout for days and peck away at it during the week. It is a nice change from my garden inventions, old milk homemade ricotta and cold oatmeal. David Mackay's focaccia has a special corner in my freezer but the minute I get a real live American hamburger and French fries delivered from Mexican Luchy's restaurant I gobble it down.

8 June 2020

This has been quite a morning already starting at 2:30 or 3:00 a.m.? Not sure. The mantle clock doesn't agree with this iPhone, lights are flashing on my Infinitum box, Alexa is yelling, "you are not connected to the Internet," and a cat outside is crying pitifully. It has got to be the Marauder who shows up, cries, and has to be told again that there is no room and board at this Inn. "We're full," as Trump would say. It is pitiful to keep hearing those cries.

I fully expect to see the turkey vultures (or TVs as Stephanie calls them) circling above my property again. Out back in the neighbor's abandoned orchard is where two cats have died (one of them mine) and been devoured already. It is scary when you imagine yourself or your loved ones becoming their target.

This 100-degree temperature I haven't seen here before as I usually leave early in April before everything dries up. The cats still come to eat, but not much and don't get as excited. They eat, then just stretch out nearby on the shady brick portal and don't move. A lot of birds I am sure are relieved.

So now suddenly no flashing lights and all systems are go. What a relief. There has been a reprieve and my only connection with the outside world has been reestablished.

It takes time to see what is in front of your eyes.
I have lots of time now.

I used to think I could only get my news from a daily newspaper. Now I get more news online than I can consume and then it floats away never to be found again. Well, I need to know what is going on to maintain a perspective other than my personal bubble and what I read about Yuval Harari's big picture.

Allamanda.

The picture on left shows how overgrown the Thunbergia vine was outside the kitchen window. Picture on right shows it cleared away. I photographed the Thunbergia vine traveling over and up the guava tree. Really, I watched it grow. So, I told Beto to move — NOT CUT — the vine over and back so it would go the other way. If you cut it, then it just starts over again. I am hoping I or he can train it away. The vine tends to kill anything it can get hold of.

9 June 2020

My second salad from my window garden.

10 June 2020

Lili and her partner Raúl searched out and found a little swimming pool for me to give to Rafaela for the kids (Manuel and Luis Alberto) to stay cool in the hot, hot summer.

15 June 2020

Louise came today to pick up my bags she will take with her to my Tucson condo where she will drop them off along with her car to leave in my garage. I want to be able to travel light when I go. Cherisse will pick her up and get her to the airport for her flight to Chicago Wednesday morning.

Like everyone who leaves she has to go for medical reasons. Her plans are really solid and safe with the help of friends. She admits it is hard to leave here where so far we seem to have dodged a bullet. My neighbors will help her get on her way. But, I needed to put my two cents in because no-one has had more experience around here with dealing with old age in an airport.

Louise all prepared to leave town.

I made her listen to my advice: Pretend you are old. You have to get a wheelchair, which is easy because airlines do not want old people to be a problem. They love making sure you are not in the way. All you need to do is ask, you do not need a certificate, doctor's note, parent's note, or even need to be covered in bandages. They whisk you to your seat without a fuss.

They will take you to the rest room, guard your bags, get you a sandwich, a newspaper, a neck pillow for a small tip. They live for tips and they wear masks. They will leave you till it is time to board then come and put you in the plane before anyone else, except maybe families with children. You can have your choice of seat, especially on Southwest.

But she was still nervous and I had answers for those questions. I gave her two adult pampers and read to her all the directions with assurances that I had researched that quality and sizes were correct. I described my personal experience using them—not good. The relief to know if you are delayed you don't ever have to use the rest room in a plane which can be crawling with the virus. I gave her rubber gloves to protect herself if she is unable to wash. Then we exchanged phone numbers so she would be able to call my neighbors in Tucson and they her. That seemed to do it.

She had brought me leftover frozen lamp chops and Hershey Chocolate powder. Well I couldn't think of a better bargain. I hate to see her leave but she needs her medicine and grandkids.

I inherited this ink sketch from Elizabeth Nuzum. Her son Kit has it in Orcas Island and is sending it to me. It is so lovely I can't wait to see it up close. It is the work of a young American assistant of Diego Rivera, Ione Robinson, born in Portland, Oregon, and who lived in Tucson in the 1940s. Elizabeth wrote a note on the back that says she wanted me to have it as a remembrance of the time when we two spent the summer looking at all the art books in Rene Solis' vast library here in Álamos.

Ink drawing by Ione Robinson.

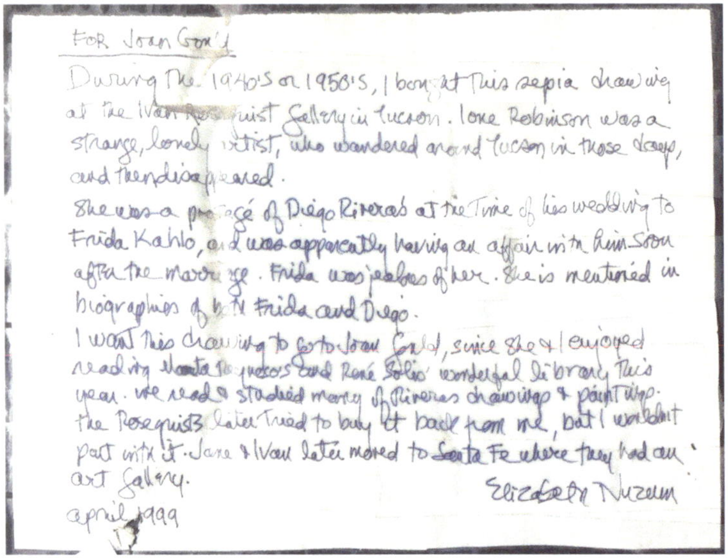

For Joan Gold

During the 1940's or 1950's, I bought this sepia drawing at the Van Rosequist Gallery in Tucson. Ione Robinson was a strange, lonely artist, who wandered around Tucson in those days, and then disappeared.
She was a protégé of Diego Rivera's at the time of his wedding to Frida Kahlo, and was apparently having an affair with him soon after the marriage. Frida was jealous of her. She is mentioned in biographies of both Frida and Diego.
I want this drawing to go to Joan Gold, since she & I enjoyed reading [illegible] and René Solis' wonderful library this year. We read & studied many of Rivera's drawings & paintings.
The Rosequists later tried to buy it back from me, but I wouldn't part with it. Jane & Ivan later moved to Santa Fe where they had an art gallery.

Elizabeth Nuzum

April 1999

Provenance — Elizabeth's note that the drawing should go to Joan.

17 June 2020

When I first came to Mexico, I felt like I was in kindergarten. I didn't have much to say; I didn't know many words, just labels. But I tried, and stumbled and laughed and everyone kept encouraging me. It didn't seem to matter when I would say in Spanish, "he doos" instead of "he does." We communicated.

Bright colors seemed so important. They were everywhere — orange, magenta, turquoise, yellow, crimson, green and blue. Too much. "But I like too much," as my friend Mary said long ago.

There was so much support, I not only was encouraged to be an artist, I began to think I was an artist. I had mentors to choose from.

There was a lot of too much: car exhaust, houses jammed together, flowers, plants in pots and cans, trash thrown around, poverty, homes inside high walls, stonework, elaborately carved cathedrals, plastic souvenirs "?," articulos de artisanias, bricks, adobes, sentiment…

Everything seemed like play. The money didn't look serious, some wasn't by my standards. Giant coins bought little, several looked alike but weren't, two weren't alike but were worth the same. There were people who work in banks all wearing the same uniform, some officials were overly officious sometimes as if they are chewing the scenery like actors.

The small Farmacias and the Abarrotes looked like classroom stores set up for kids to play in, so small. People with fruit and vegetables sat on the streets adoring what they sold; making pretty piles. Funerals of the poor people were replicas of those I used to imagine when I thought of burying a loved pet as a child.

Everything seemed more intense and simpler. I found back to when I was in kindergarten.

Lluvia de Oro, Rain of Gold (Golden Chain) tree in bloom in Fala's yard. The book Rain of Gold *about the Mexican Revolution in the Sonoran region was a blockbuster. June is when it blooms which is why I never got to see it. When we first came we never left but after a few years we learned how to avoid the summers. That was before AC.*

18 June 2020

Adenium, Bird of Paradise, Pandorea, Allamanda.

I guess I am here in ÁLAMOS for the duration of this Pandemic. I have watched most of my girlfriends leave successfully one after another to Pacific Grove, CA; Portland, Oregon; and Alaska, Embarrass, Minnesota, Chicago, Illinois, Montana, Sonoita, Tucson, Show Low, AZ; and northern New York.

Patricia, Ann, Suzanne, Louise, Melanie, Myrna, Jean, and Jude. There are still many of us left but we all have the rains to look forward to and so far, few cases of the virus.

I don't like what I hear about Tucson right now and I vividly remember last year sitting by my sliding glass door in Tucson, hoping to see desert animals and rain. Rain never came to my yard except for three-minute dribbles. Now I can expect to be drenched, even drowned if I stand under my many canales. I will be able to watch leaves, vines, and trees growing and flowers opening. More wild bouquets to pick even though many of the flowers here are short-lived when picked. It won't matter, I can photograph them before they expire. They will never tell. Andy Goldsworthy taught me that trick.

I am free, though it might appear I am imprisoned by some. Earle has left me independent and for the first time I can play without having to consider anyone, take care of anyone, live with anyone. This is a new experience for me and I better take advantage of it. Because my favorite thing to do, I have learned, is to play.

I remember when I lived in LA in the thirties playing in the ocean, getting beaten up by the waves, rolling in the sand, just generally becoming a mess that needed cleaning up and a nap. I loved everything about the ocean, no fears of tides, sharks, temperature changes, stinging nettles or rays, pollution, waves. A long time ago.

From left, sister Lois, brother Lynn, and Joan on Hermosa Beach in the 1940s. Middle: From left, sister Lois, a friend, and Joan, about 1938 at Balboa Beach, CA. At right: with her parents stopping off in Pago Pago in 1930 on the way to Los Angeles from Australia.

Then there were paper dolls and blocks, I would create houses, clothes, families, towns. Clothes were important even then.

My playmates were always the boys across the street. They had the most fun. They ran, climbed, planned, and fought fig wars, and were always racing around. I was not allowed to go there for long periods which was probably a good thing.

I don't remember playing much after that till Gene Riggs and I opened the Back Door, our crafts gallery in Paoli, PA. Then I would spend all my free time hunting for art. I didn't know anything about art but I thought I knew it when I saw it or at least grew to know a lot about what was beautiful to me. Gene was not interested in giving instructions.

Joan and friend Billy Gilliland off to kindergarten in 1935 in Los Angeles.

Then came Handmade Paper play. Somehow I knew I needed to learn to make paper. Like you have heard actors and artist and scientists and writers say they always knew what they had to do in life. I watched a famous Italian ballet dancer on YouTube the other day describe how when he was three he knew he had to be a ballet dancer. He was adamant.

I first met Judy Ingram at The Back Door. She was a handmade paper artist. That was in the 1970s. I knew then that was for me but had to put off getting lessons for 40 years till I retired and came to Mexico. One day during my papermaking class in San Miguel D'Allende I asked the professor if it was okay if I did something, forget what, on my own. He said, "You can do anything you want!" That's play! I was off and running.

Oh yes, I remember now playing in the kitchen trying out new things. It was fun making dinners for parties but the most fun was playing with Jello desserts for three kids. What amazing concoctions I came up with to keep them interested. They probably hate the sight of three-color Jello to this day. And getting the neighbor kids to cut up all my garden vegetables to make gaspacho. The drudgery I wanted to avoid. Remember playing means you are not focused on pleasing anyone, only yourself.

So now I have this COVID Sentence where I have a chance, maybe my last chance to play to my heart's content. Working to create this blog does it for me now.

This time I have help, which makes it ever better, with Megan's taste and graphic arts skills. We are trying to make this beautiful, fun, and informative. Enjoy.

20 June 2020

David MacKay.

I walked up to Solipaso at 5:15 this morning to see if I could do it when it was relatively cool. David MacKay was giving a bird-watching talk. The walk takes about 20 minutes on a slightly inclined paved road. I did it but was glad to get a ride back 2 hours later as the heat was building.

David magically caused Black Vented and Streaked Back Orioles, some Varied Buntings, Greyheaded Tanagers, and Ashbrown Flycatchers to appear that I have never seen at my place down the street. He used his bird calling app and maintains stores of bird food.

It is truly the most divine nature resort you could ever want to visit. Elizabeth Nuzum bought the land in the 1960s and spent years designing her dream of a straw bale house, utilizing her Mexican son-in-law and his family, to create out of the thorn forest and huge boulders a property that was to become a world class retreat.

Chacho and family members while building the straw bale house.

A giant Mexican fig tree stood in the center of it for several hundred years but was lost in the hurricane of 2008. Elizabeth sold it to the MacKays before she died. They have since developed it into what you see.

Fig tree, now gone, near Elizabeth Nuzum's original straw bale house.

El Pedregal Nature Lodge and Retreat Center, originally built as a straw bale house.

22 June 2020

Teri and I once reminisced about the 1980s when she and Elizabeth introduced me to Elsa Klensch on TV, the fashion maven. It was heaven for an hour every Saturday. Recently I introduced her to Fashion Designers 2020 on YouTube which I just discovered. I was up till 8:00 PM watching their fall/summer lines. Better than Michael Jordan, Bruce Lee, and Sergei Polunin, the Russian ballet dancer I have been watching.

Now I get to imagine prancing down the runway wearing outlandish outfits and choosing however many I want. Teri complimented me on one yesterday. It was my 25-year-old Donna Karan from the sale rack of the discount store south of Santa Fe. I seem to have lots of Donna Karans. Old old old, second hand.

I am now watching fashion for 2 hours in the afternoon and have picked out the dress I want to buy. Actually, I want two of them, one for Megan's birthday and one for myself.

Remember in the past when I really wanted something expensive I would always buy it for Megan first because I never believed I should buy anything expensive for myself. Except ice skating lessons and the mini fish sailboat. She asked me once if that boat was hers, how come I took it to Arizona with me?

Earle always accused me of being reckless with money. He thought I wasted it. You were never supposed to spend money, money was only for making more. Wonder what these dresses cost anyway and IF they would ever buy two of them.

23 June 2020

We filleted all these but there are hundreds more coming. I'm usually in Tucson in June and miss this bounty.

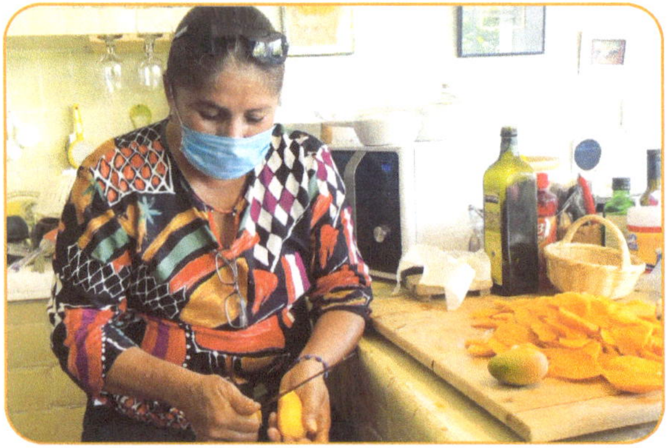

Fala filleting mangoes every other day.

Mangoes ready for the freezer.

The beginning of the mango harvest.

Looks like a painting by Cezanne.

It is 4 a.m. and I am battling with Amazon in bed in the casita and can hear, actually feel mangos hitting the pavement outside every few minutes. If I had to peel and fillet them in addition to gathering all that fall AND battle with Amazon I would not survive this Pandemic.

Belladonna Lily.

Actually though, I realize I am one of the lucky ones with not many cases here (12), lots of friends keeping watch, AC, a functioning well, ATM 3 blocks away, restaurant deliveries, Beto to blow away all the dust and leaves (I am paying 93-year-old Manuel to stay home so I don't have to watch him move leaves around with his ancient broom), and redirecting massive amounts of Thunbergia vines from climbing to the tops of all my trees and stunting their growth.

The reason I am battling Amazon is because Sandee in Tucson is collecting everything I order to load into her Mexican worker's truck in two weeks when he will drive with my recumbent stationary bike down to Àlamos on his way to his family's ranch nearby.

This is a dream come true which I may actually pull off. Chuy has offered to meet him 40 minutes outside of town in his truck in case he is not allowed to enter Àlamos.

12 *Number of known COVID-19 cases (reported to me) in Álamos week of June 26, 2020.*

28 June 2020

Limes.

My new COVID/ Water cocktail, eight a day in the fanciest glass I have left till I run out then I will rob somebody.

Everything isn't Edenic in The Garden of Eden. I should know, I live in one. It is always too much, too little, not ripe or rotting, or needs watering.

Millions of limes when I just got too old for Margaritas. Millions of plátanos when the ones I froze have turned brown in the freezer. Millions of naranjas after the birds got to them first. Millions of Meyer lemon real still ripe after I made all the meringue pies, lemonade, dressing, zest, ices, sherbet, pudding, soufflé, sole, liqueur, custard, frosting, cake and tried to give them away.

The really worst part of living in an Eden is having a glut. When you cannot give them away because you live surrounded by Edens just like yours. I am talking mostly about mangoes, limes, and grapefruit. Birds and rats are sick of them. The retired folk I live among in Mexico have been advised by their doctors that grapefruit has an effect on their medicines. The old folks home across the street has no one well enough to benefit from gluts.

Also, there is no room to plant anything in an Eden ever… does an Eden not evolve? All the ground is thriving with green green and tall tall. You are limited to living with what is there. It is as if your Eden dropped from the heavens. Everywhere is shade. In order to grow, plants have to get tall to find the sun, as if they were never planted, just dropped full grown. It sounds like heaven but what if you want to plant something new? Not a chance.

14 *Number of known COVID-19 cases (reported to me) in Álamos week of June 28, 2020.*

3 July 2020

21

Number of reported COVID-19 cases in Álamos currently.

5 July 2020

I am still waiting for rain … the forecast keeps changing and now I see five future days predicted even though no predictions have come to pass for two weeks. Will we have a deluge? Well, that means lots of video of a deluge. Everything is getting really greener with just air water. I expect to see green cats soon.

What is Mia doing, is she upside down and stuck? (See photo.) Dan the cat (not shown) has arrived to check on me AND any birds dumb enough to be walking around in puddles — I'm just guessing that's what he is doing. I would like to demolish the casita front wall so I could see even more while sheltered but have to settle for what still is just fine.

Twenty-nine cases Fala announced when she came in this morning to fillet the mangoes. No deaths.

Thunbergia.

27 *Number of reported cases in Álamos currently.*

8 July 2020

Wow! Woke up at 3:30 a.m. to the sound of rain and thunder, glorious thunder. I jumped up and madly started making coffee, cut the AC, pulled all my plugs out of their sockets (except for the coffee), peed, opened the door, checked to see where all my important items were buried in my bed: passwords, iPhone, remotes for TV, AC, land line, closed pen, paper scraps and my three New Yorkers that came all at once, and dry skin cream.

I grabbed the curtain and stuffed it into the file cabinet so I could see what was going on outside. I remember telling workmen 33 years ago to put the concrete base for my mattress in the corner opposite the curtain-less picture window so if I ever got old and sick I could watch the rain. Then I drove to the border to escape the summer heat. When I got back in cool November the concrete bed was ALMOST in the corner. I thought my life was ruined. It was slightly off center... how was I going to manage??

Now I can lie back and enjoy the little stream of rain water trickling down the wall from a leak in my cathedral ceiling.

July 8 indoor salad material.

Raining!

Bird of Paradise, Day Lily, Adenium, Gloria, Bougainvilla, Allamanda, Carolina Wild Petunia.

13 July 2020

You may remember little Manuel, the little swimming pool swimmer. He is one of two nephews Fala is caring for during this pandemic. Their mother is a nurse and the whole family is protecting the boys. It was wonderful to see how close the family is. They hang out at her place now that it has been upgraded but I suspect they would have done that if nothing had been changed.

Manuel with two calves under his care.

Chuy and I conspired to take this downtime to to figure out what Fala's inherited house (used to be mine) needed.

Amazing how it had deteriorated over the years when I was not paying attention and she was not complaining.

34 Total | 14 Active | 20 Recovered | 0 Deaths

Number of reported cases in Álamos currently.

We cleared away space around the house, installed fencing and a stone portal with a roof overhang supported by Fake cantera pillars (my contribution), built a barbecue, comal and new outdoor laundry and rose garden. Then brought in many bougainvilla plants to hide the fencing. We replastered and retiled the inside and improved the plumbing. And finally brought in camping cots (to accommodate the revolving family members) and a large plastic cattle watering tank to store rainwater and serve as a swimming pool for the young Manuel and Luis Alberto.

I see the house now filling up with assorted members of her family I guess with shifting responsibilities. She cannot be there all the time as I have to be tended to occasionally.

Now I see that the herd of 20 cows she has been investing in have birthed two calves. They are lucky Manuel has taken over their care. I suspect they will be looking sharp as well as thriving.

15 July 2020

I am wearing whatever I run across now both inside and outside, and might even wear it inside out, over and under things. Just changing all the time into stuff that feels good, doesn't match, amuses me. Street clothes to bed, bedclothes for lunch and dinner. I like to raid my several closets looking for something different. And now I find that when venturing out in the yard to do laundry or pick up the thousands of mangoes for Fala to fillet I am stripping down, standing under the shower outside to make moving easier in this heated humidity. Soon the pool will be full of rainwater and I can splash in buckets. My iPhone weather forecast promises nine days of rain starting Friday. I may regret what I am wishing for. Hope the casita floats. I could use some new buckets as mine are crumbling in the sun.

Last year I went crazy when I found a mother lode of handmade baskets. I bought maybe 20 just cause I like to look at them. Now I use them all moving around the yard and back and forth from the casita up to the kitchen carrying what I need back and forth. They are full of fruit, weeds, scraps of paper, pens, a cell phone, nail file, empty coffee cup, crackers, Gum, pills, eye drops, New Yorkers... did you know that if you subscribe to the *New Yorker* in the states you can call them, explain you are going to Mexico on vacation and they will send the magazine to your new address free of charge? For six months, a year? Sometimes I get three at once down here. That is fine with me. They don't go out of style. Not this pandemic year though. No magazines have arrived.

Mexican Creeper and Allamanda.

17 July 2020

Chuy just came over to take the old lady on her first spin in a month. We went to Fala's house so I could get pics of the new work. We have been at this for four months. When I asked him how much I have spent, he said around $4,000 American, which includes both the outside and inside.

The plants are already taking over and I see many things I have thrown out and given to her growing at her house. Cuttings of all my plants are flourishing. A glut of zinnias are blazing away. Where did they come from? I will have to ask her for seeds to plant in my yard. She needs to be reminded she is my gardener too.

I took photos of all the steps. When I wasn't looking, I gave permission to build almost all of them. There will soon be four. The original brick house we bought 20 years ago had one. Then I said OK to two more and now I guess I just agreed to another. All in such a small space… it is OK though as they are cheap and so darling.

The stone patio was built with my insistence to provide resistance to black summer mold which mars all other surfaces during the summer rains. This is one of my successful attempts to insist on a standard of beauty influenced by a lesson of Bruce Riggs, master stone mason. After applying cement wash down gently with the spraying of water to allow the stone to stand out.

From left, the original stone steps built 25 years ago, a tiny round step and detail of the stone patio, and recent steps which should have been made round.

18 July 2020

Bird of Paradise, Ponderea, Adenium, Thunbergia, Day Lily.

39	19	20	0
Total	Active	Recovered	Deaths

Current number of cases as reported to me today.

19 July 2020

I got this card from Megan and Ken in the mail, three months late for my birthday in Àlamos. But I have been working hard every day since despite the heat and pandemic to make each day ridiculously fabulous.

Elizabeth Nuzum had a large new bouquet on the table she sat beside every day when she held court in her white garden. chuy (have no idea how his name was spelled), her gardener with an amazing nursery, brought it when he came to work each morning. I must have absorbed that custom as I am doing it for myself now.

Elizabeth Nuzum receiving at home. The bouquet is a gift from an admirer. She had many admirers.

She lived in her own amazing garden full of flowering vines. I remember I spent many hours researching and hunting down those vines for my own garden—another aspect of my creating for myself her habits that I have admired.This developed into a project together with Barbara Kirbach to publish a book called *The Flowering Vines of Àlamos*. We almost did it. I researched and photographed while

Barbara researched and wrote.

Then events conspired to cause the project to die on the vine, so to speak. But we did determine there were over 50 flowering vines in Àlamos from all over the world. When I was in the Bahamas once I was amazed that there were flowering vines which we had in Àlamos; the same thing happened in Hawaii. I know Àlamos women who have traveled the world actively transporting exotic plant material to their gardens: Buck Mills, Elizabeth Nuzum, Suzanne Chartrand, Diana Roslee, Babs Watson, and the only one still living, Stephanie Meyer.

I now have 12 of those vines in my garden and I find myself making those bouquets for myself. They provide an endless supply of flowers which if you are not fussy you too can have daily bouquets… Many do not last more than a day, if that. Sometimes I have to clip a bloom or two from low hanging blossoms as I walk the streets of Àlamos. Sometimes I ask first.

When I got tired of my vases and flowers, I conspired to visit the gardens of friends asking to be allowed to cut flowers in their gardens and use their vases. They receive the bouquet of their flowers in their own vase and I get the photograph. Andy Goldsworthy gave me that idea.

21 July 2020

Pandorea, Bougainvilla, Mexican Creeper, Allamanda.

23 July 2020

A few unrelated thoughts and images today. Fala just came to rescue me from tons of cucarachas, dust, dishes—and brought me this bouquet from her garden and her sister.

He is a class cat to whom I will finally give a full name, Don Dan. In Mexico Don is a word for respect, like Sir. He is always alert to what is going on, checking to see that all is going well with his girls, choosing to accompany whichever one amuses him at the time to meals, licking their faces and whatever to calm them down, quelling arguments, alert to all movements of birds and the deterioration of rotting mangoes, making sure all lizards are tailless, and sleeping up against the metal garage door to guard against intruders. He doesn't like me to open the door for fear I will let something in. It worries him to be so exposed. He continues to lie there watching for street dogs. He chooses to never cross to the outside. I think he prefers the privacy of his own territory. We don't seem to have any more marauders, this humidity may have killed them off. He does his roaming only after dark God knows where he goes.

Don Dan. I think he is getting ready for a major role on Broadway.

25 July 2020

This morning, a bit hazy, but this scene was brown a month ago. I am so lucky to be alive to see this.

The landscape is awake from the monsoon rain.

40	20	?	?
Total	Active	Recovered	Deaths

Number of reported cases, partially updated.

27 July 2020

These past few days nearly finished me. Three weeks ago, I decided that I would just stay in Àlamos till the Pandemic is over. Conditions in the U.S. and Arizona are so terrible I really do not want to be there. I don't want to get that close to Trump.

So, I have been remotely cutting ties. But three things have made that decision difficult: My beautiful recumbent stationary bike is there, my new 5' x 8' painting by James Kevin Wilson, which I have never been close to is there, and I am paying monthly for a purified soft water service I cannot turn off. Then it hit me.

While my short-term memory is largely gone, which I guess gives free rein for ideas to ricochet and crash into each other now, amazingly, fresh ideas have room to explode.

One did. I could have my bike brought to Álamos! Cheaper and easier than trying to get myself to Tucson and back. It might be years before I could fly anywhere from Tucson. It never rains in Tucson and there is a chance of a forest fire in Tucson. I know more people in Àlamos. I don't have a maid in Tucson.

So I have been putting in place the logistics to make this happen. Hera, the Mexican American who does construction in Tucson for me and my neighbor Sandee, brought my two new white couches in his truck to Àlamos four years ago when he drove down to Hermosillo to visit his parents.

Wait, wait... it gets better. He agreed to do it again! In a pandemic? But Mexicans are really close to their families I know. Well, he agreed and I decided it was so important I could offer a lot of money. Money I cannot spend flying places.

Then Sandee suggested why not have him bring things from Amazon south? Well, yes!

I remember one day encountering Peter Combs in the plaza when he was supposed to be in the hospital in Montana near the end of his life and asking him how he got here, he said, "I charted a 6-passenger jet for my nurses and myself." I have never forgotten that thinking outside the box. He did what he could do. This was my equivalence.

Hera and family. They had a great time accomplishing my mission. Since they came without masks they had to stay out of the house. I served them mangoes in the garage.

Good idea. After Sandee volunteered to receive packages from Amazon and pick up my full box of mail I was off and running. It was so easy to buy everything I might need for a year. But maybe some things I already had in my condo, things that were lonesome there. Perfume and lipstick in the refrigerator. My Ninja. My heating pad. A bag I sent up a month ago with Louise.

My Tucson bike. Safely in Álamos now.

Sandee didn't seem to mind the bother. I know the feeling, getting Amazon packages is such fun, even when they aren't yours. But especially when you don't have to pay for them. She recommended seeds for the coming vegetable garden in October. I loved having her there going thru my condo noticing things maybe awry? I left in October of last year. Better than having to go there. I even got my grandson to agree to take my new giant painting if I don't make it back. He called it awesome, which is all I needed to hear. I hope that means he likes it cause the size is awesome.

So I fretted and worried for weeks that this could really happen in a pandemic. Chuy and Hera exchanged photos of trucks, license plates, and cell phone numbers. We tried to think of everything. What if the authorities in Àlamos won't let him enter? What if there are holdups on the highway? Does he need papers from the presidente in Àlamos? Chuy said not to worry, he could meet him and put everything in his truck.

Well, come the day. He was late? He was in San Carlos? Probably sightseeing at the beach? Hera tried calling from the highway, no response? Probably no cell reception? Then came a call from 20 miles out of town saying he was held up by the authorities. Chuy got the call and gave them his best imitation of Àlamos authority in Spanish. "This truck is bringing in a stationary bike for 90-year-old resident Joan Winderman, prescribed by her doctor along with medicines and masks for

Àlamos residents. The call was taken by Cecy Anaya's sister who was on duty at the time. She knows me. I may be famous as the oldest American woman still alive and Cecy is my hairdresser. Age is revered here, truly.

So, they let them through. What a relief to see them but what a shock to watch five people unfold from an American licensed truck stuffed with a bike and boxes. I was shocked. I would not have let a truck from Tucson that full of people through even on a mission of mercy. Tourists are not allowed in.

When the bike was unloaded these darling people pictured stopped eating the mangoes I gave them and reloaded the truck for takeoff. I gave them money to stay the night out of town and get back across the border. I didn't want them to suffer from doing this. It is such a miracle to feel safe and supplied for the duration hopefully.

So, this morning I slathered my bike with [sanitizer] gel and pedaled for an hour while watching a Michael Jackson video, almost without effort.

Now I don't have to chance walking on cobblestones in this heat.

Thanks to everyone who helped make this happen. I have to rest now and try not to think of any more good ideas.

29 July 2020

Arugula! I have no arugula seeds now and did not know they would germinate in the hot summer. So, I am picking off five leaves a day for my salad. Hope it is enough to sustain life. But I can supplement with plenty of limes, mangoes, oregano, thyme, marjoram, rosemary, and mint by mixing it all with flour and a little water (wonder what color that will be) and baking It in a bread pan.)

I notice another shoot out there that might be snow pea or string bean. I threw enough orange peels out there so maybe I can expect a tree or trees soon?

Volunteer plant — new freebie growing in my empty vegetable garden.

5 August 2020

I have been waiting for the other shoe to drop: bad news. It is bad but could be worse and I need to report it because it is part of the story, but, opposed to the situation in HAMILTON, I am alive to tell my story.

Rosy, Chuy's wife, had to drive 4 hours south to rescue her sister in Sinaloa when her other sister went back to Atlanta leaving Abby alone. While there, their brother died and the large family, some from San Diego came to Sinaloa for the burial. They all came down with COVID-19 afterward. Hospitals were full there so Chuy got the best hospital in Navojoa to send an ambulance to bring the two back to San Jose hospital. It is not full because most people cannot afford it, no charity cases. They probably cannot afford the ambulance either.

So, Abby was diagnosed with a mild case and has been brought by ambulance to Àlamos and is now locked in one of Chuy's six empty casitas, fully equipped with TV, bath, sitting room, kitchenette, AC. I am eyeing one of the others. The hospital provides portable oxygen and on-line daily doctor visits.

Rosie's condition is not good but improving some. At this point she is on oxygen but not intubated. Her lungs have been affected. The prognosis is another 10 days in the hospital.

Chuy is doing everything he can think of to make things

Podranea, Allamanda yellow and plum, Thunbergia, Mexican Creeper, Mandevilla, Bird of Paradise, Veracruzana.

better. First, he got a haircut. The first time I have seen that. That is what I would do, I think. Now he is driving everywhere putting out fires, buying medicine, groceries, etc. Keeping busy as usual.

I used to benefit from all that, now I have to step up, not complain and try to be encouraging. Just as my new phones have died, I got an unusually gigantic electric bill which I am trying to find the cause of, my new 50-inch TV with ROKU does not speak my language, the tech who installed it has not come back to install my old one in the kitchen, I don't know how to tell if my refrigerator is leaking, etc. Small potatoes right?

I am focusing on the good news: my super exercise bike was delivered to me along with my Amazon purchases with Sandee's help, I now have more cornmeal than anyone in Mexico, I can now begin sprouting broccoli, and kale seeds, I get to make a new bouquet every day, and nobody got COVID from that delivery so far.

And I am 90 years old so I will not have to live on the edge forever. There are pluses to being forced to live in the now. And I get to doubly appreciate life by writing about it.

6 August 2020

I am busy hunting for good news this week to balance the bad. While I was reading in bed yesterday, I noticed a shape vaguely familiar near me on my velour bedspread. But I couldn't make it out… a dried leaf? But maybe not. So, I decided to get my tweezers from among all the gizmos I sleep with, picked it up and took it into better light. Still not sure as it seemed pretty dried up so I got my magnifying glass. Ahhh, just as I thought, a medium-sized scorpion long dead. Dead is good but how come, from where and when? I think when Marta comes again I will have her pick up everything, shake it out and look underneath everything again and maybe more often.

That comes under the heading of scary good news.

Yesterday Fala showed up (she does that now twice a week and pitches in with whatever is going on. I leave her in the kitchen masked and bustling.

She noticed my tablecloth was badly stained, my attempt to do laundry had stalled, washed clothes were still in the washer but the dishes had all been put away. She got busy, like Megan used to do when I was floundering, and put everything right again.

Then I remembered the old days and asked if she would make lunch for me — pescado empanizado con papas suaves y ensalada usando las plantas voluntarias de rècula apuera y las plantas en la Ventana.

That was delicious good news.

Podranea, Allamanda yellow and plum, Thunbergia, Mexican Creeper, Mandevilla, Bird of Paradise.

8 August 2020

Rescue arugula, window-grown Little Gem lettuce, mango, avocado, almonds, bacon bits, and olive oil and lime dressing.

Salad greens in pots.

49	?	?	1
Total	Active	Recovered	Deaths

Known COVID-19 information in Álamos, from Friday the 7th.

12 August 2020

Alexis, my new tech tutor.

I had a long session with Alexis yesterday, my new tech guy. It wore me out. He is indefatigable, speaks good English, and is darling. At 22 he has an at-home-in-Mexico call center job with the American company Grub Hub and lives nearby.

Recently he was bumped up from working with clients to drivers. I can see that his skill and personality are perfect for that job. Also, that I am not the only no-nothing, bumbling, needy American he has ever run across.

I struggle to explain what frustrates me about trying to do impossible things with a bad memory and no computer background or vocabulary. He looks at me blankly then delivers a navigation path to a solution much like a robot. And smiles expectantly waiting to see how I respond. Yes, I get the same feeling of not being judged as when I took a math course online. It was such a relief to be able to learn over and over at my own speed without judgement.

I learned a bit about why he is where he is, working at home monitored by his private school educator mother and electrical engineer brother. His brother said he was crazy and he said he had been a bad boy. Well, I have known something about that kind of charmer.

COVID-19 local status as reported to me today.

Now that my indoor Little Gem lettuce is getting scraggly, I dumped it after refrigerating the last leaves. I had Beto soak and clean out all my clay pots to prepare for the winter white geraniums soon to arrive in November. Now I will try to subsist on Kale sprouts. I just tried planting five seeds of kale, parsley, basil, eggplant and bok choy to see if I can get something going outside early. I see a few tomato, basil, arugula and eggplant volunteer shoots out there. Nice to have the time to notice these things.

Rain Lily or Belladonna Lily, Gloria, Allamanda.

16 August 2020

What a relief that I get to have Cecy cut my hair in my house. But she is close and it only takes five minutes and I try to shower her with gifts. She is fussy about her clients and has been known to cut off the tardy and crabby. I understand because part of the reason I like her is to get to hear her stories about her family, sons, and politics and gossip in Àlamos IN ENGLISH.

Latest haircut from Cecy.

She always looks so fashionable and attractive. And has a way of making us look so much better than we are. Especially us old girls.

Her hobbies now that her sons are grown are decorating fabulous cakes that sell for more than I would pay and mascetas planted with a variety of cactus which she decorates with images of darling Mexican senoritas. These too are prized among her clients.

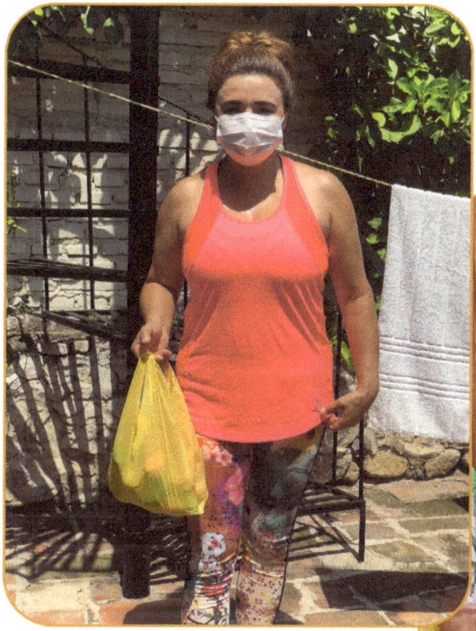

This is Cecy bringing mangoes down from my roof which she noted on Facebook she made into mango ice cream. She can have anything growing around here unless there is not enough for me. I make mango ice cream also.

Window container garden at Cecy's.

18 August 2020, Part I

It is distressing what is happening to us, and we are the lucky ones. The ones with choices, but that we can choose to mess up even more is even sadder. I realize it is easier for me because I don't expect to be around and so I can make easier choices like, what do I want to do before next month? But if you need to plan for a lifetime...

We have to see this though in terms of millenniums, or centuries, because it is not about us. Think how many bullets we have dodged since we were born; wars, atom bombs, other pandemics like Ebola, what good lives we have had compared to most; think how many people now don't have even a shelter, a job, money, and maybe are losing the chance for an education. We are so lucky. We may even live to take down the asshole and that will be something to look forward to. Maybe I need to make a new list of things to look forward to in these bleak times.

Trying to keep a stiff upper lip.

RESEARCH

- Take down Trump hard and the people who support him and who he trumpets and supports
- See a woman VP or even President in our backward country
- Watch all the people who denied global warming and the importance of wearing masks in a pandemic die. More importantly, reverse the warming
- The widespread distribution of a vaccine to protect from COVID-19
- The next book of Yuval Harari
- Another beach house experience or just floating in salt water
- Seeing my new painting (by James Kevin Wilson) in town
- Take down the NRA hard
- Solve the immigration problem
- Cure our Supreme Court Judge, Ruth Bader Ginsburg
- Pass free Health Care which includes free abortions
- Free preschool for all
- New CCC-like program to employ workers to upgrade our infrastructure
- Make marijuana sales legal with a program like we have for liquor
- New laws to make physician-assisted care to end lives legal in all states

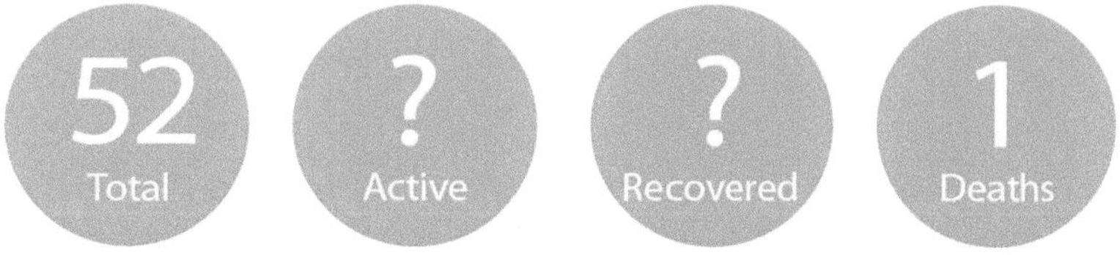

COVID-19 local status as reported to me August 15.

18 August 2020, , Part II

It is my passion, trying to understand who and what I am so I can try to understand what is going on around me. I grew up convinced something was wrong with me. What? I had no idea, so I looked everywhere. I enrolled at Ohio State University in 1948 to study Psychology. That seemed to be the best place to start. It was only a start. All through my first marriage and three kids I was looking for the answer. Then a second marriage, more college and teaching, and still looking.

Now at 90, I feel comfortable that what was wrong was that I believed what people said about me. I wasted all those years. I was always listening for an answer. So, when I heard the head of the Reading Department of Temple University say in the 1970s, "Our brains work to create order out of chaos," I was ready to absorb Harari's pronouncement that the human brain creates stories and that is what has made us so powerful.

So, my passion is to absorb what I can about what is going on around me and to try to understand what I can learn about myself to better respond to what appears to always be evolving.

That means in this age of Pandemic to decide for myself best practices (while learning from those who are also trying), as most of mankind is not doing a good job of it. Looking for answers from people like Harari scans the big picture, and encourages any and all efforts to understand, experiment, make changes, create new ways, and overcome the danger of what appears to be a big drop-off ahead.

Things were dire BEFORE the Pandemic, nuclear war, global warming, and artificial intelligence.

19 August 2020

This came about when I decided my frozen assorted sliced peppers needed to be used with leftover sliced onions and fried eggplant so I could clean out the refrigerator. All I had to do was refry everything in a little olive oil, add my Chicken Better than Bouillon and some water to my trusty Ninja and whirl away. Didn't need to strain it much. It is lovely. I think I could subsist on this for quite a while. Although I would run into the danger of never wanting to see it again after a week, I bet. Oh well, there will be other collections piling up in the coming days. The trick is to have a Ninja which transforms anything, lots of waste material, and a kiss of good olive oil (as Earle often uncharacteristically would say).

Thank you, Sandee for suggesting that you could run into my condo, capture my Ninja and some lipstick, and put them in the truck delivering my doctor-prescribed stationary bike to be delivered to Àlamos.

23 August 2020

Night Blooming Cereus, Adenium, Day Lily, Limes.

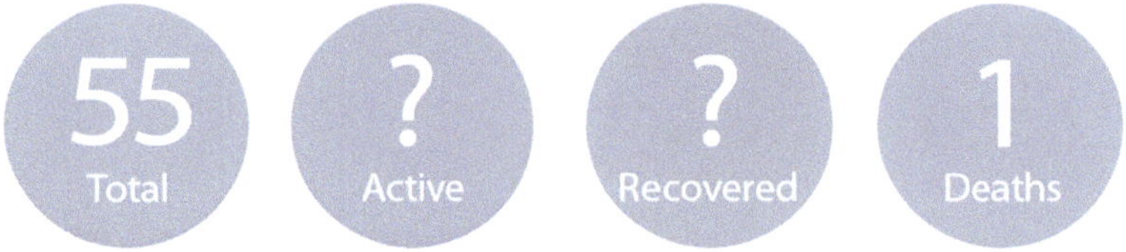

COVID-19 local status as reported to me August 23.

25 August 2020

Do cats eat shoes? Well, I think the recently titled Don Dan did. This is only on circumstantial evidence that I am condemning him, but he was at the door next to the flip flop when I opened it in the morning.

What the cat dragged in.

I am new to having cats and I thought one of the joys was that they don't run off with things, tear up things, eat things that aren't generally considered food, bark, knock over things, and are easy to push out of the way. Especially if you don't ever let them inside — outdoor cats.

Well, yes, they do eat shoes — at least one brand new, expensive, black, rubber, OEFOS flip flop that had just arrived by truck from Tucson. It was to last me for the duration of the Pandemic.

Don Dan was at my casita door this morning and I was thinking that after the rainstorm last night he might have needed some comforting. Then when I couldn't get my shoe to stay on, I looked down and a part of it was missing.

I am having a hard time trying to control my reaction to this. Maybe I will just quietly say to myself, "That's one."

Update Sept. 19:
I am expecting to need all of these in the future! Sometimes we get Amazon deliveries where you would never expect them. Now I'm ready to do battle with Don Dan the next time he attacks.

Replacements of my new favorite shoes.

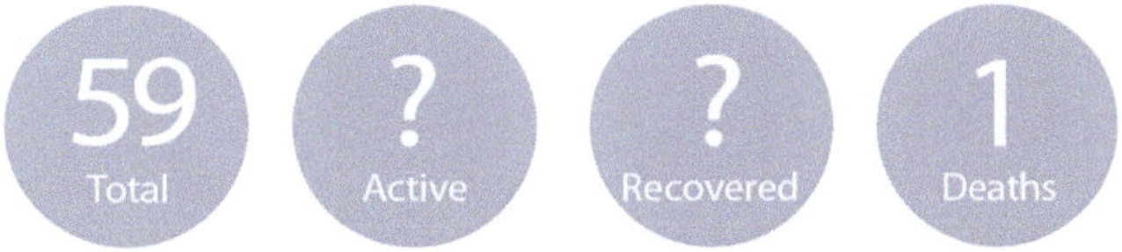

COVID-19 local status as reported to me August 26.

31 August 2020

Freshly drained ricotta cheese.

An amazing thing happened this morning. I discovered that I could make ricotta out of milk that was sour. Don't know why I threw away so many half gallons of milk here in Àlamos that had turned up sour even when the sell-by date had not been reached. I never questioned their uselessness. Maybe because I was pissed.

This morning while pissed because I had two new half gallons both sour, I put them on the stove, turned the burner on high, forgot them and let them boil. I hadn't hovered over them worriedly either. Then I dumped in some vinegar without measuring and the result was fine.

Actually, I operate this way a lot, my modus operandi. I tell Fala when I see her eyes widening with a you-know-what look that this is *una experimenta*. She wasn't here.

Now it tastes fine, would be better with lemon which I don't have, and it seems a little less tender. It didn't need much draining, ten minutes, but tastes fine. So now I have to find more uses for it as this will soon become a staple in my refrigerator.

I better stop taking my calcium pills.

This week I visited Fala's house to see how the exterior painting is moving along.

Bouquet of Periwinkle, Indian Jasmine, Podranea, White Mountain Flower, Rain Lily, Duranta Erecta, Allamanda in an old Paul Bernhardt broken casserole.

1 September 2020

Raphael Angel Arenas Wong and his dog.

It was so cool and only raining softly when he came by, so we took advantage of a chance to visit outside sans masks. I have wanted to visit with him for a while, Raphael Angel Arenas Wong. He is one of the Mexican friends I have made here who speak English, a real treasure for me as I am mostly dependent for background and gossip on what I can pick up from these conversations.

Magpie jay on a saguaro. Photo by Chuck Babbitt, 2020.

He took Lisa and Chuck on a guided nature tour when they were here last year. Chuck's photo of a magpie jay in a cactus during the trip was a prize winner. We talked about the two baby magpie jays he had just found in the wreckage of a tree that had collapsed recently. If they survive, they will be tough to keep in a cage.

He told me the story of how he came to be half Mexican and half Chinese. He has never been to China, doesn't speak Chinese, and has no close Chinese relatives here. If you saw the movie Sonora, made mostly on the trek from Sonora across the border up into Papago, or now Tohono O'odham territory, you would have seen what happened in the U.S. early in the last century when the Chinese were forced to leave Mexico, and what happened to Wong's grandfather. He never met his grandfather but his father went north later to look for him around San Francisco and never returned.

His family has remained in Mexico and become educated and prospered with no knowledge of the Chinese culture they are descended from.

We had a great talk while becoming delightfully wetter and wetter. No noseeums also.

2 September 2020

I recently purchased what I thought might be an interesting book because I am always looking to understand more about psychology, especially about power. I have no interest in poker. Also, I was curious about what another woman might have learned about poker. So, I ordered *The Biggest Bluff* on Amazon by Maria Konnikova and it arrived with my truckload of Tucson purchases a few weeks ago.

It was amazing. She is Russian with a background writing professionally for magazines, including the *New Yorker, NYTimes, Slate, Scientific American,* etc. She won an award in 2019 for Excellence in Science Journalism. While writing this book she became an international poker champion and winner of $300,000 in tournament earnings. She graduated from Harvard and received her Ph.D. in Psychology from Columbia University. When she started, she knew nothing about poker.

After finishing the book, I decided one of my neighbors here might be interested in reading it, as he has long been a member of the original Àlamos poker club and he was a close friend of Earle's. He loved the book and recommended that I loan it to others.

I heard from another resident when I offered to loan him the book that for the last 30 years all the poker club guys considered Earle had been consistently the best player. All this time I thought Earle was just bragging. You never knew with him. He told me once that he borrowed a book from Bernie Abramson and that was how he learned to play. Maybe Trish still has that book.

Luìs Àngel Castillo Grajeda, my newest computer tutor.

Not much to say about Luìs yet except that he is attentive, patient, knowledgeable about computers, iPhones, new TVs, Roku, Fire Stick, remotes, English, has a printer, and he listens with a sense of humor. To say nothing of his being in his 20s, a teacher, charges less than I'm willing to pay, married with a boy, and darling. He has a tendency to inexplicably vanish, though.

I explained that I did not want to be told he would arrive at 3:00 p.m. manaña, when he is just saying manaña to see me happy. It doesn't make me feel good because I feel terrible when I have to sit in the garage in this heat by the door so I will hear his knock, then he doesn't come for hours if at all. I want to be called and told he will be here in one half hour, so if I forget, I can take a quick shower, dress, find my pen, computer, phone, remotes, key, and sit by the door with plenty of time because he won't actually be there in a half hour.

That's the way you get kindergarteners to admit things. Let them know how much their behavior hurts you. You can ham it up and it works even better. But this is ingrained in our locals and helps to smooth out relations. It is also fun to play that game yourself so you never have to feel rushed, or responsible. Any excuse is a good excuse. I like pretending to be a Mexican.

6 September 2020

I looked up recently near where my orange tree is supposed to be and realized no oranges were in sight, only a solid mass of green leaves. The jungle had grown out of control again. One Amapa tree had burst into five which had been heading skyward for the last 20 years.

Periwinkle, Podranea, Bougainvillea, Adenium, Coral Bells.

Watching plants flourish is exhilarating until it isn't. It happens when you are not looking. You keep wishing for more more more. Then the undergrowth starts to die out and change, branches stretch over and across the roof, and it gets ever darker under there. It is a slow but relentless process, almost sneaky. Of course, I am talking about this happening in plain sight over a long period of time. So, it is not really sneaky.

But once I noticed that there were fewer oranges developing, strange leaves showing up, and little rain hitting the path below I began to look up more when passing underneath. The Orange tree had grown way above the roof while at the same time being almost smothered by the even taller young Amapas.

Baby Amapa tree.

And this year is the first time I have noticed thousands of Amapa seedlings all over the place. My iPhone plant identifier app claims they are Mulberry trees. That can't be right! I puzzled over that identification for weeks before it dawned on me that a Mexican hardwood invasion was taking place under my radar.

I called Bony Hurtado, our only local palm tree trimmer. He came soon after with a helper, his ancient machete and a snarl of well-used rope, no ladders, no saws. He is amazing to watch scooting up trees, throwing his legs over branches, leaning against and lassoing trunks, hacking away in a whirl of thrusts.

All of this effort on a day so hot and humid I had to get photos during fast forays between shots and gasping dashes to air-conditioned couches. I forgot how old I was but it was apparent after it was over.

Now he is gone. I gave him money to scoop up every leaf and branch from the yard and haul it all in his tiny truck to the dump, in one trip of course, decorated and held down with all the old bricks and stones and Royal palm fronds which have been languishing outside my garage door for a month hoping someone would steal them.

The cats were outraged as they watched from various vantage points wondering what to make of all the commotion. Or that was what I think they were doing. They must have been scared though, they are never a group of three.

So, now I am looking out at my suddenly revealed giant Orange tree looking slightly embarrassed at being revealed so brazenly. Oops! Have I stripped away too much?

Three amapas gone. Orientation: Looking toward the house through the newly cleared space between giant mango tree on the left and giant orange tree on the right.

8 September 2020

Rosa and her sister Abby (left) during a party in March 2020.

Bulletin: Chuy has announced that Rosie and her sister Abby have been released from their quarantine and are considered cured of COVID. They have been moved to inside the main house and are working to regain their strength. The danger of being susceptible to whatever else is going around remains because of their weakened condition, though. So, good luck to them as they make use of their new oxygenator and Nustep T4R exercise bike. They have been through a lot.

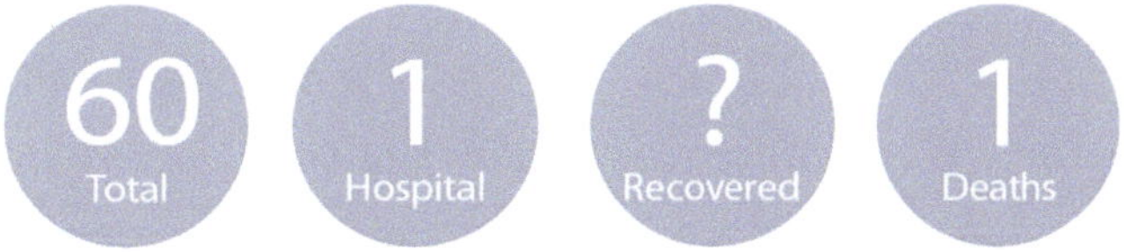

COVID-19 local status as reported to me September 9.

Gloria, Allamanda, Podranea, Maidenhair Fern, and first Meyer Lemon. Pitcher by Bruce Riggs of Pennsylvania.

Fallen limes.

10 September 2020

Everything blooms then fruits, then the fruit drops, then the leaves drop, then I am told the limes do it all over again if there is rain. We will see. I am experimenting again. Rather than rake up the limes and put them in the trash or on the compost pile, I am raking them up and leaving them under the tree. If a growing lime tree uses what is in the soil to grow then the fruit and leaves that fall must contain something the tree needs so why not leave the limes and leaves under the tree. I only use one lime a day. I have three trees and more poking their heads up. I could ask Stephanie if I am right but want something to hope for. Of course, I don't do the raking here.

14 September 2020

Mart B. Riggs, 1899–1990.

Grampa, (my father), had a few talents he chose to ignore, as not worth talking about. Below are photos of some I managed to capture when he wasn't looking. The ironwood Phoenix, as he named her, was the best one. When I insisted it was a work of art, he said, "I didn't do anything, it was already there." You heard that, remember. Mother said, "You can have that, he didn't even finish it." This epitomized the war they were engaged in at the time.

Long hours spent in the 100-degree Coolidge, Arizona, garage heat drove him to have his way with maybe 33 ironwood letter openers he carved by hand and passed around to family and friends. That was before slow mail went out of style; now they are just precious souvenirs of those days.

The crazy stone and metal sailboat came about after he saw how much I loved knocking over and falling off my beloved (half Megan's) Mini-Fish sailboat at Apache Lake (east of Phoenix). I still cannot keep the iron sail upright. He didn't drill the groove in the stone deep enough. Maybe it was taking too long or it was too hot out there. But I never heard him complain about the heat. I don't think he had AC.

I think there are still some handcrafted ironwood buttons around.

Works by Mart Riggs (1899–1990). Ironwood Phoenix sculpture, stone and metal sailboat, ironwood letter opener, and wood stool.

Podranea, Allamanda, Mandevilla, Gloria, Adenium.

22 September 2020

66	?	60	1
Total	Hospital	Recovered	Deaths

COVID-19 local status as reported to me September 22.

28 September 2020

The newly named Dolly.

This is a confused story. Mìa came after Dan and is his blood sister. Well, her mother's blood and someone else's. Her other sister came with Dan first, but died mysteriously.

Mìa shit on my bed after I tried to protect her when Dan tried to tear her apart the day she appeared, and I have the video to prove it. I mean, the video is of him chasing her. They were six weeks old. Shameful.

She is now one of his lovers. For some reason, she is mean to everyone but Fala. Fala thinks that all animals are God's children, though. Mìa has earned my enmity to this day.

Dolly — to whom I never gave a name before — showed up with her sister or brother (who died before I determined which), and robbed the feeding dish, along with others. Adobe walls cannot keep out alley cats. Not Don Dan and Mia who were given to me by our museum director and could be considered upper class.

So then, in order to create some semblance of decorum in my family here, I captured the much later named Dolly and took them all to be fixed. This has relieved my mind but I still have to patrol the premises and keep my collection of rocks handy. The present marauder is yellow with a bobbed tail. Have to keep straight who is in and who is out. Nobody else is going to be fixed or welcomed in.

So, now we have the newly named Dolly and I cannot wait to greet her each morning with "Hello Dolly." She is the only one who meets me at the door on time and who doesn't seem to be out catting around all night. And she is so eager to be popular that I call her that ironically.

I don't have much respect for her as she shamelessly wiggles herself in front of Dan to attract his attention and backs down whenever Mìa hisses at her. I never found those behaviors to be attractive or effective. And I am not impressed by anyone who is ALWAYS punctual. Nor who looks too needy.

11 October 2020

BREAKING NEWS — Panteon Damage To Gravesite

Door of nicho ripped off, mask slightly marred. Friends of Earle D. Winderman may have been celebrating before Día los Muertos. His mask will be replaced by votive candles in the future.

14 October 2020

I called Julio the plumber when I noticed small puddles of water on the kitchen floor for three mornings. We hadn't had any rain. He solved the problem.

We are all patched up now but it was scary. We had a mini geyser right there in the kitchen. After carefully removing six bricks we discovered a water pond. I guess after 33 years even copper pipes wear out. We are lucky we can't sink and we now have it patched, but it was touch and go.

Julio to the rescue!

68 Total | ? Hospital | 60 Recovered | 1 Deaths

COVID-19 local status as reported to me October 1.

Clerodendrum, Bougainvilla, Jasmine, Gloria, Allamanda. Angels by Cammy Nuzum.

15 October 2020

Recently, I have been watching all the interviews of Stephen Sondheim on YouTube now that everyone is celebrating his 90th birthday. He and I have some things in common. I am inspired by his work, not only the music and stories but particularly his lyrics. I know something about what he knows about Art, his process.

The Art of Songwriting with Stephen Sondheim, interview on YouTube.

COVID-19 local status as reported to me October 15.

Low tide at Wells Beach, Maine, 1958.

When I look back on my life, I see how Art has become very important to me. Maybe my first brush with it was when I lived at the beach in Wells, Maine, for two years in the fifties. At that time that beach had little sand, mostly ocean-washed stones. I walked it a lot and studied those stones and collected them and brought them home and studied them again, and spent a lot of time choosing the most beautiful ones. And then when I had whittled those down to first, second, and third place, I put them on pedestals with spotlights shining on them. I have taken them with me wherever I went for the last 70 years.

Joan and Megan on the sea wall in front of their home in Wells Beach, Maine, 1955.

Rocks gathered from Wells Beach, Maine, in 2001 by Megan.

Joan and Megan on the front porch of the Wells Beach house.

Choosing what was beautiful was what I was doing. It was wonderful work I considered important. I went back recently. It has all been erased. No stones, only sand. Hundreds of houses where there had been only 20. Mine has vanished. I think I was teaching myself about beauty then. I was immersed in it.

Much later after many moves, I ended up living in the Philadelphia area and starting a gallery in the 1970s with my sister-in-law who is an artist. She thought it would be fun to start a crafts gallery along with our other duties as homemakers and mothers of a total of seven children. I was again immersed in choosing beauty to bring to the gallery. I thought I saw it everywhere. Then changed my mind, then tried again and again. Fortunately, some of my choices were sold and so I was free to make new choices. That experience lasted five years.

Well, it has become part of me. Many future choices were influenced by those experiences. As the years went on, I ran into an expression that felt like it belonged to me. I didn't understand it at the time but I made a large sign and wrote it in big letters and hung it high in my elementary school classroom. "What you choose is what you are; what you love you yet shall be." I would look at it often and wonder what it meant and why I loved it so much.

Last week listening to Sondheim's lyrics to "Sunday in the Park with George," I realized that in depicting the creative process in Art he was describing something I knew about. The following quote is sung by George Seurat's mistress, Dot, near the end of the show, as he struggles painfully with his doubts.

> "Stop worrying where you are going. Move on. If you can know where you are going, you've gone. Just keep moving on. I chose and my world was shaken, so what? The choice may have been mistaken, the choosing was not. You have to move on. Look at what you want, not at what you are, not at what you'll be. Look at all the things you've done for me. Opened up my eyes, taught me how to see. Notice every tree. Understand the light. Concentrate on now. Let others make that decision, they usually do. You keep moving on. Look at what you have done, then at what you want, at where you are, at what you'll be."
>
> — *Stephen Sondheim*

6 November 2020 Dia de los Muertos 2020

Celebrating Dia de los Muertos in the Panteón de Álamos at Earle's sofa.

Archway of paper flowers.

I hopped a ride for my annual tour by train of downtown Àlamos.

Dia de los Muertos 2019

From the Baron's Ball in 2019, Joan with her niece Lisa Barnes, Lisa's partner Chuck Babbitt, and friends. Photo by Chuck Babbitt.

COVID-19 local status as reported to me November 6.

10 November 2020

I am feeling frazzled, as I guess we all are. But I am being buoyed by some thinkers I have found on YouTube and in books that are available to me here in Àlamos by people who are attempting to make sense of the radical changes we all are experiencing right now with politics, global warming, AI, the rise of an expendable class, nuclear proliferation, and the Pandemic all of which are upon us. I need to concentrate on what might be in the future after this political conflagration which we as people have brought on ourselves.

The good news I guess is we won the election; the bad news is this is only the beginning. We are not prepared. We are not ready. I have to know more about what is going on so at least when I die I might be ready to leave. A very religious person I once knew told me I was brave not to have his faith in God and heaven.

I want better information about what is maybe what I will be leaving behind when I die and maybe then I will feel better about becoming dust. I don't need to be brave. He has since died and I think he probably didn't go to heaven. But he doesn't know that.

I dig into all this because if I want to understand the game; I need to know what to root for and the rules AND to keep out of trouble so I can manage to be informed enough to land on my feet or at least avoid getting cut down by what's coming. Change is coming even faster than we have been predicting. I want to know what that will be like.

Here is a list of who I have been listening to or reading. It reminds me of those guys, my father's friends, I listened to in our living room in Los Angeles in the 1930s when I was trying to decide who knew the most about what he was talking about. I have had to drop a few people along the way as they disappointed.

- **Yuval Harari** from Israel tops them all right now even though I haven't heard him say much about the Pandemic, he has prepared me to see the latest thinking describing a world picture of the past and future of mankind and beyond. I like the idea that my brain constructs order out of the chaos surrounding me so I can create a better story that I can believe in.
- **Ian Bremmer**, a political scientist, is all over YouTube being interviewed and has written many books. The one that helps me understand why Trump has had such an influence on so many Americans is one that I consider the clearest explanation of what we all need to understand right now about his 70 million followers. US vs THEM and the failure of Globalism is the name of that book. What is it that has made Trump so popular? Why is it so many follow him while it is obvious to I hope more people who think he has been a danger to our country.
- **Peter Freihan**, a geopolitical thinker, who lectures and writes books about among other things the effects of geography on the success of civilizations and countries economically and politically. His lectures and books are thrilling to hear and read. He does not talk much about Global Warming or the pandemic though. He predicts economic winners and losers.
- **Michio Kaku** is a theoretical physicist who has written many books, his latest is "The Future of the Mind," which I am about to read.
- **Victor Gao**, "The World after COVID 19," Deng Xiaoping's English interpreter
- **Mohamed El-Erian**, Beijing, "The Only Game in Town"
- **Fareed Zakaria**, author of many geopolitical books, "Ten Lessons for a Post World Pandemic"
- **YouTube Munk dialogs from Canada**

- **Malcolm Gladwell**, YouTube and many books
- **Stephen Meyer**, "Evolutionary Biology"
- **Russel Brand**, comedian, actor, writer
- **Lawrence Krause**, theoretical physicist and cosmologist
- **Robert Wright**, "The Evolution of God"
- **Christopher Hitchens**, "God is not Great"
- **E.O. Wilson**, Harvard entomologist, studies of ants
- **Sir Ken Robinson**, Doctor of Education
- **Mohammed El Erian**, "The Only Game in Town"
- **Barack Obama**, "A Promised Land"
- **Shoshanna Zuboff**, "The Age of Surveillance"
- **Dr. George Friedman**, YouTube political science professor
- **Stephen Fry**, actor, comedian, and writer
- **Elon Musk**, businessman, industrial designer, and engineer
- **Sol Kahn**, Kahn Academy
- **Jeff Bezos**, Amazon.com
- **Walter Isaacson**, author and biographer
- **Steve Wozniak**, co-founder of Apple Computer, Inc.
- **World Science Festival**, panel discussions, found on their YouTube channel

So, these are my cast of tutors for now who are helping me put together a story about the world. They keep me from dissolving into a puddle these days. It is exciting to be on this busqueda while hunkering down in Álamos.

I remember wishing in Copley High School in 1946 that I would have a dramatic life. I guess I have created a dramatic life — my own — even though I didn't know at the time what a dramatic life was. I invented one which feels like it belongs to me.

22 November 2020

Gift of painting by Robyn Tinus to me from Ray and Nicole Latham upon the recent sale of their property. Rafaela who has worked here for 25 years and owns six cows approves. Painted about 2010.

COVID-19 local status as reported in Álamos as of November 22.

Robert Spinrad, Earle's brother-in-law.

8 December 2020

Earle and I were driven by his son Mike around Palo Alto one week in August 2009 to visit Earle's brother-in-law, Bob Spinrad, who was suffering from late-stage ALS while confined to his home. Late in the afternoon Earle's sister asked me if I would like to take a walk around the neighborhood, so we did. First, we passed Sergi Brin's house. I knew little about him at the time and wasn't impressed. This was a small, very private collection of beautifully landscaped, comfortable suburban homes linked by wide-curving sidewalks. The architecture didn't stand out. No surprises, but the next one not only stood out but you could miss it if you weren't paying attention.

Portion of interview with Steve Jobs found on YouTube.

We walked past what she referred to as Steve Jobs' house. I had heard of him by that time and even owned a Mac but didn't know much about how to use it. Immediately, I was stunned by the unusual plantings in his front yard. You would expect them to be beautiful but they knocked me out. The front yard was full of dwarf apple trees. I didn't think to take a photo at the time.

Bob Spinrad told me a story about the day Steve Jobs came to his Xerox PARC lab in Palo Alto. Bob was the director, working on GUI — graphic user interface — among other things. He showed Jobs around all three of his projects at the time.

101

COVID-19 local status, total of cases reported in Álamos to me as of December 9 .

Pandorea, Petunia, Clerodendrun, Coral Bells.

12 December 2020

Though I say I am not going out again, I did go for a walk in Parque La Colorada with Lili, Chuy's daughter, and her kids. This is right behind Chuy's house. Miles and miles, 112 hectares. I needed guides, 'cause I could get lost.

A 36-foot bamboo pole in my yard, taken down and stripped by Carlos, with inset details.

15 December 2020

Carlos Valenzuela, my new gardener, is replacing my four-year-old trellis for the Thunbergia vine. We are going to replace it piece by piece so we don't have to collapse the whole vine. It is wonderful to have a stand of bamboo replenishing itself on the premises. I like to watch them turn from a gorgeous green to yellow, and then gray very quickly. He knows about bamboo and Japanese gardens from photographs on the Internet. He and I will get along I can see.

17 December 2020

David MacKay's smashing vegetable garden at El Pedregal, our beautiful Eco Hotel outside Álamos.

104

COVID-19 local status, total of cases reported in Álamos to me as of December 17.

20 December 2020

The neighborhood is coming back to life. Everybody is alive and well.

Column 1: Ted Glattke,
Chuy & Grandkids,
Janet & Kelly Hale,
Jean Glattke.

Column 2: Bill & Linda Adams,
Jay & Ann Gallagher, Douglas Reynolds,
Melanie Dreisbach & Richard Schain,
Peg Franken.

Column 3: Jude Conroy, Beatrice Sak,
Richard Schneider, Myrna Ruffner.

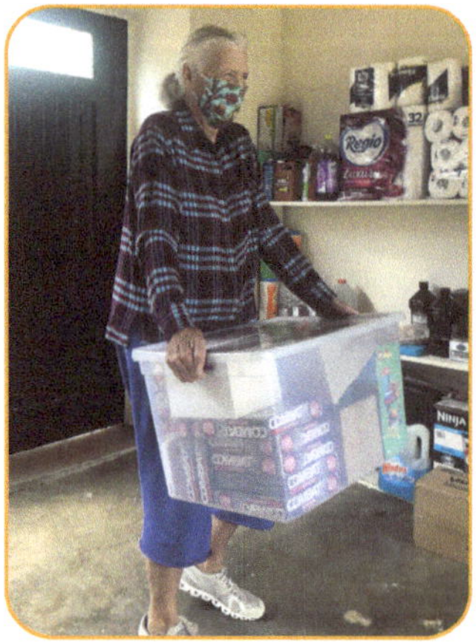

Louise made it down to Álamos. She brought me all the Amazon purchases and mail that I could get Sandee to store in my garage in Tucson.

25 December 2020

I am trying not to have too merry a Christmas this year. Save it for next year. I am staying behind this door for Christmas and behind these walls till I get a COVID shot.

109 Total | ? Active | 3 Deaths

COVID-19 local status, total of cases as reported in Álamos to me as of December 31.

1 January 2021

I got carried away at Christmas and managed to arrange to buy a 40" smart TV and a year's worth of WIFI for Rafaela (which meant her whole family benefits) including two tablets for her 18-year-old niece and 12-year-old nephew, so they can keep up with their schoolwork. Lili and her partner Raul got it all installed. That is how I avoided shopping and wrapping this year. Nobody is complaining.

Parents of Rafaela.

Look at the smiles on the faces of her parents. I panicked when I saw that big TV in her little sala. I was afraid I had disrupted her family by overdoing things but I guess not. When you have help in Mexico you can take on or be overtaken by a whole family, if you are lucky.

Rafaela and her nephews.

New bougainvilla-covered fence.

I want to live here, it is so magical. Rafaela is going to have to cut back the foliage periodically, I think, but will finally have the privacy and safety she has always wanted. Many of her family members seem to be living in that greenery off and on. And I see there are two bikes garaged inside. Two dogs also. The portal floor is stone and can be washed down whenever the plants need watering or the giant swim tub needs emptying. Notice her two papaya trees. I think she is must be serving papaya every morning for breakfast. I hope to get some someday.

Off to Tucson to get my first COVID shot.

Copa de Oro, Petunia, Clerodendrun, Gloria, Pandorea.

134

COVID-19 local status, total of cases as reported in Álamos to me as of January 8, 2021.

Off to Tucson for COVID shots.

143 Total 4 Deaths

COVID-19 local status, total of cases as reported in Álamos to me as of January 12, 2021.

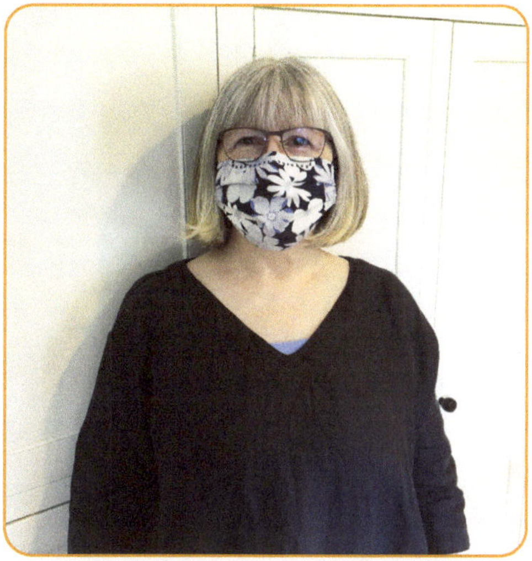

Blog Administrator and Designer

MEGAN PETERSON

Solebury, Pennsylvania, Joan's daughter.

https://grafinis.blog/alamos-diary-2020-joan/

Painting *Primary Folklorico*, by Millard Davidson.
Reproduced by permission of Swickard's Hacienda de los Santos, Álamos.

Printed in the USA
CPSIA information can be obtained
at www.ICGtesting.com
LVHW070004060823
754251LV00002B/16